Her Father's Voice

Shane O'Reilly

I0141044

methuen | drama

LONDON • NEW YORK • OXFORD • NEW DELHI • SYDNEY

METHUEN DRAMA
Bloomsbury Publishing Plc, 50 Bedford Square, London, WC1B 3DP, UK
Bloomsbury Publishing Inc, 1359 Broadway, New York, NY 10018, USA
Bloomsbury Publishing Ireland, 29 Earlsfort Terrace, Dublin 2,
D02 AY28, Ireland

BLOOMSBURY, METHUEN DRAMA and the Methuen
Drama logo are trademarks of Bloomsbury Publishing Plc.

First published in Great Britain 2025

Cover design: Sarah Moloney

A catalogue record for this book is available from the British Library.

Library of Congress Control Number: 2025945574

ISBN: PB: 978-1-3505-9781-5
ePDF: 978-1-3505-9782-2
eBook: 978-1-3505-9783-9

Series: Modern Plays

Typeset by Mark Heslington Ltd, Scarborough, North Yorkshire

For product safety related questions contact
productsafety@bloomsbury.com.

To find out more about our authors and books visit
www.bloomsbury.com and sign up for our newsletters.

CREATIVES

Creator/Writer/Librettist	Shane O'Reilly
Composer	Tom Lane
Director	Annabelle Comyn
Conductor	Elaine Kelly
Set and Costume Designer	Joanna Parker
Lighting Designer	Stephen Dodd
Sound Designer	Philip Stewart
Director of Photography/Editor	José Miguel Jiménez
Producer	Pádraig Heneghan/Lovano
Production Manager	Pete Jordan
Stage Manager	Miriam Duffy
Assistant Stage Manager	Rachel Spratt
Costume Supervisor	Thérèse McKeone
Sound Engineer	Kevin McGing
Projections Engineer	Daniel Staines
Associate Producer	Daniel Culleton
Associate Producer	Ois O'Donoghue
Assistant Director	Kate Russell
Assistant Costume Supervisor	Maeve Smyth

CAST

Claudia	Fiona Bell
Frank	Colin Campbell
Darragh	Seán Campion
Marion	Rhiannon May
Carol	Amy Molloy
Sarah	Ellie Rose Fenlon
Sarah	Ella Nora Kucheruk
Ciara	Chloe Brown
Ciara	Charlotte McCluskey

Shane O'Reilly

Shane O'Reilly is a playwright and actor living in Dublin, Ireland. Recent writing includes: *Her Father's Voice*, *Gold in the Water*, *swansong*, *windowpane*, *The Water Boys*, *Näher…closer – nearer – sooner* and *FOLLOW, FARM & CARE* (co-created with WillFredd Theatre).

Tom Lane

Tom Lane has composed for many of Ireland's foremost theatre, dance and opera companies. He has been nominated for six Irish Times Theatre Awards, including Best Opera for *The Stalls*, *Front of House* and *Flatpack*, and Best Soundscape for *The Haircut* and *Whitby*.

Notable recent work includes composition/sound design for *IMPASSE*, choreographed by Mufutau Yusuf, which premiered at Dublin Dance Festival and toured internationally, composition/musical director for *The Weir* (Abbey Theatre), composition/sound design for *The Blackwater Lightship* (Verdant Productions), composition for *The Tragedy of Macbeth* (Almeida Theatre), composition/sound design for Yaël Farber's *Hamlet* (Gate Theatre/St Ann's Warehouse, NYC) and Annabelle Comyn's *Look Back in Anger* (Dublin's Gate Theatre). He composed music for Hannes Langolf's physical theatre piece *Unruhe* (Theater Trier) and *The House Trilogy*, a new series of operas commissioned by Cork Opera House. In 2019, Tom created *The Haircut* with writer and director Wayne Jordan. The show was revived to critical acclaim in 2025 at The Ark, Dublin.

Tom also composes music for concert performances. Recently commissioned works include *Nocturne* for the National Symphony Orchestra of Ireland, *Earth* for the Esker Festival Orchestra, *Trio* for the Picorlino Ensemble, and *Refractions* for the Banbha Quartet.

Further credits include: *The Loved Ones* (Rough Magic/ Gate Theatre/ Tour), United Fall's *Girl Song* by Emma Martin, Annie Ryan's *The White Devil* at Shakespeare's Globe, Ballet Ireland's *Giselle* choreographed by Ludovic Ondiviela, *The Seagull* for the Corn Exchange, *Romeo and Juliet* at the Gate Theatre, and *Twelfth Night* and *Oedipus* at the Abbey Theatre (nominated for Best Sound Design, Irish Times Theatre Awards).

Annabelle Comyn

Annabelle is an award-winning theatre director and artistic director of Hatch Theatre Company. Her freelance work includes: *The Sugar Wife, The Wake, Hedda Gabler, Major Barbara, The House* (Irish Times Theatre Award for Best Director), Pygmalion (The Abbey), *Girl On An Altar* (The Kiln/The Abbey), *Ravens* (Hampstead Theatre), *Our New Girl, Look Back in Anger, The Vortex* (The Gate), *Evening Train* (The Everyman), *Asking For It* (Landmark Productions, The Everyman, The Gaiety, Birmingham Rep.), *Crestfall, Helen and I* (Druid), *A Number, Blue/Orange* (The Peacock), *Dancing at Lughnasa* (Lyric Theatre, Belfast).

Her opera credits include: Beethoven's *Fidelio* for Irish National Opera (The Gaiety) and *Dubliners* in an adaptation by Arthur Riordan (Wexford Opera Festival), both nominated for TITTA for best opera production.

Hatch's recent productions include the Irish premiere of *Escaped Alone* by Caryl Churchill in a co-production with The Everyman for Cork Midsummer Festival (CMF) and the world premieres of Coetzee's *The Jesus Trilogy* by Eoghan Quinn in collaboration with Comyn for Dublin Theatre Festival(DTF), *colic* by Eoghan Quinn for DTF at Pavilion Theatre, *To The Lighthouse* in an adaptation by Marina Carr (in a co-production with The Everyman, Pavilion Theatre and CMF), and *The Talk Of The Town* by Emma Donoghue (in a co-production with Landmark and DTF).

Joanna Parker

Joanna Parker designs sets, costumes and video for theatre, opera and dance. Based in London, her works have premiered in the UK, Europe and the USA.

Recent engagements include: *The Cave, Translations* (Set), *iGirl* (Set), *Walls and Windows* (Set), *On Raftery's Hill* (Abbey Theatre, Dublin); *The Barber of Seville, Glass Human* (Glyndebourne); *The Other Boleyn Girl* (Chichester Festival Theatre); *The Flying Dutchman, Requiem/After Tears, Les Pêcheurs de Perles* (all also Video Design) (Opera North); *Aida* (Opera North, Montpellier); *Turandot* (Opera North/ Teatro Nacional de Sao Carlos); *Floating Island* (Theatre Rites, Burgtheater Vienna); *Carmen, Precipice* (The Grange Festival); *Much Ado About Nothing* (Globe Theatre); *The Noise of Time* (Complicite); *American Buffalo, The Misanthrope* (Young Vic); *After Darwin* (Hampstead Theatre).

Stephen Dodd

Stephen Dodd is an award-winning lighting designer for theatre, dance and opera. He trained at The Samuel Beckett Centre, Trinity College Dublin. Stephen won Best Lighting Design Irish Times Theatre Awards 2022 for *Volcano* for Luke Murphy/Attic Projects and was nominated for Best Lighting Design Irish Times Theatre Awards 2023 for *An Octoroon*, Abbey Theatre.

Recent lighting credits include: *The Cave, Youth's the Season -?, The Quare Fellow, The Long Christmas Dinner, An Octoroon* (Abbey Theatre), *The Jesus Trilogy* (Hatch Theatre/ Once Off Productions), *Scorched Earth, The Prometheus Project, Volcano* (Luke Murphy/ Attic Projects), *Dark Days Need Ceremony: Soft God* and *King / Shrine, Night Dances, Birdboy, Girl Song, Dancehall* (United Fall), *Beckett sa Chreig: Guth na mBan* (An Taibhdhearc with Company SJ), *Il Teorema di Pasolini* (Deutsche Oper, Berlin/Dead Centre), *GATMAN!* (Cork Everyman), *Good Sex, To Be a Machine 2.0, Beckett's Room,*

Hamnet, *Chekhov's First Play*, *LIPPY* (Dead Centre), *What We Hold* (Jean Butler/Irish Arts Centre, NYC/ DTF), *Animals* (Louise White Performance), *Morrígan, Heart of a Dog* (John O'Brien), *A Thing I Cannot Name*, *Orfeo ed Euridice* (INO), *The Here Trio*, *I/Thou*, *Wrongheaded* (Liz Roche Company), *Crossing Skin*, *Dances Like a Bomb*, *The Misunderstanding of Myrrha* (Junk Ensemble), *The Examination*, *The Circus Animal's Desertion* (Brokentalkers), *Eastland* (The Collective) and *Company* (Company SJ).

Philip Stewart

Philip Stewart has created music and sound for a broad range of media including theatre, sound installations, dance, film shorts and documentaries.

Recent theatre credits include: *The Jesus Trilogy* adapted by Eoghan Quinn (HATCH & Once Off); *The Sugar Wife* by Elizabeth Kuti (Abbey); *Girl on an Altar* by Marina Carr (Abbey); *The Steward of Christendom* by Sebastian Barry (Gate); *The Book of Names* by Louise Lowe (ANU); *To the Lighthouse* by Virginia Woolf (HATCH); *The Approach* and *Howie the Rookie* by Mark O'Rowe (Landmark).

He has been nominated for an Irish Times Theatre Award for his work on *The Early Bird* by Leo Butler (Natural Shocks) and *An Enemy of the People* by Henrik Ibsen (Gate Theatre).

Pádraig Heneghan/Lovano

Lovano is the producing and general management entity for Pádraig Heneghan. Since 2012, he has worked with some of Ireland's leading independent artists in creating new work. He is currently working with Shane O'Reilly (*Her Father's Voice*, Dublin Theatre Festival 2025, *Gold in the Water* (2023 and Irish tour)), Jean Butler (*What We Hold* (2022–2024) and previously with Emma Martin/United Fall and Michael Keegan-Dolan.

In 2022, Lovano co-produced *Walking with Ghosts*, written by and starring Gabriel Byrne, with Landmark Productions, in Dublin, Wexford and Broadway. Other work with Landmark includes *Backwards up a Rainbow* (Rosaleen Linehan and Conor Linehan, 2021), general managed *The Weir* (Dublin – a co-production with Kate Horton Productions, 2025) and three summer seasons of a new production of *Once* at the Olympia Theatre (2015–2017). He general managed projects for Riverdream Productions (*Heartbeat of Home* – its world premiere and international touring (2013?2019)) and large-scale projects for Tyrone Productions in Croke Park.

Previously, he was Deputy Director at the Gate Theatre, Dublin, and oversaw its touring to leading international festivals (Edinburgh, London, Sydney and New York) and transfers of its work to the West End and Broadway.

Thérèse McKeone

Thérèse McKeone is an award-winning designer who has worked extensively in theatre, television, film, fashion and the corporate sector. Previous costume design includes productions for Thisispopbaby, Performance Corporation (nominated for Best Costume Irish Times Theatre awards), Longroad Productions, Shinawil, Theatre Royal, Coisceim, Opera Machine, Rex Levitates, Complex Productions and deputy costume designer on the 2006 Ryder Cup. Supervision work includes Irish National Opera, Landmark, Druid, Ouroborus and The Gate.

Rachel Spratt

Rachel has a BMus from Technological University Dublin. She started with Irish National Opera and has worked as an ASM on many of their shows, including *Tosca*, *Der Rosenkavalier* and *Cosi Fan Tutti*. She was ASM with b*spoke theatre company's touring production of *Dinner with Groucho*, which went to Dublin, Belfast, Oxford and London.

She has worked as a stage manager for Irish National Opera's *Breathwork* and *Music, Magic and Mischief*, as well as The Abbey's touring production of *In Real Life*.

Daniel Culleton

Daniel Culleton is a freelance producer, having worked with companies such as Lovano, Exit Pursued by a Bear, Jaxbanded Theatre and Play Not Funny.

Credits include: *What We Hold* (dir. Jean Butler), *Our Little World* (dir. Louise Lowe), *Spliced* (dir. Gina Moxley), *HYPER* (dir. Ois O'Donoghue) and *Who Robbed Annie Queeries?* (dir. Connie Henry & Niall Keane).

Ois O'Donoghue

Ois O'Donoghue is a theatre maker, producer and co-founder of Jaxbanded Theatre. Her debut play *HYPER* premiered at the 2023 Dublin Fringe Festival and was nominated for the Fishamble New Writing Award and George Fitzmaurice Award, before touring to Edinburgh Fringe Festival 2024 where it received a nomination for the Popcorn New Writing Award. In 2024 Ois was named Director of the Year by *The Arts Review* for her work on *HATE F%#K* by Jodie Doyle. Her latest original piece *FREEZE* was featured in Landmark Production's *Theatre For One: This Ireland* at Cork Midsummer 2024, receiving 5-star reviews from *The Irish Times* and *The Irish Examiner.*

In a producing capacity, Ois has worked on projects such as *Lost Lear* by Dan Colley (Edinburgh Fringe Festival 2025), *The Maker* by Dan Colley (Dublin Theatre Festival 2025), *Content* by Ross Dungan (Dublin Theatre Festival 2024), *Dream Factory* by Lords of Strut (Dublin Theatre Festival 2024), *The King of All Birds* by Martha Knight (Bealtaine Festival Toronto 2025), *Night Dances* by United Fall (Edinburgh Fringe 2022), *What We Hold* by Jean Butler (Dublin Theatre Festival 2022) and *Gold in the Water* by

Shane O'Reilly (Project Arts Centre/Mermaid Arts Centre 2023).

Kate Russell

Kate Russell is a Dublin-based director and theatremaker from New York. She is the Founding Artistic Director of Threadbare Theatre Workshop and a Princess Grace Award winner. Kate trained at The Lir National Academy of Dramatic Art, Shakespeare's Globe, and Rutgers.

Fiona Bell

Fiona's theatre credits include: *A Misanthrope* (Smock Alley Theatre); *King Lear, Hamlet, Who's Afraid of Virginia Woolf, The Father, Tribes, The Price, Boston Marriage, The Vortex, An Enemy of the People, The Real Thing* (Gate Theatre, Dublin); *Pygmalion, Major Barbara, A Midsummer Night's Dream, Oedipus, The Dead, Medea* (Abbey Theatre); *The Last Return, Leaves* (Druid Theatre); *Leaves* (Royal Court); *The Field* (Gaiety Theatre); *Richard III, Henry VI Parts 1–3* (Royal Shakespeare Company/Young Vic); *Dancing at Lughnasa, The Master Builder, Mirandolina* (Royal Lyceum Theatre, Edinburgh); *The Misanthrope* (Chichester Festival Theatre), *Cyrano de Bergerac* (Communicado Theatre Company/ Almeida); *Macbeth, Mate in Three, Good* (Tron Theatre, Glasgow).

Her film and television credits include: *Only Child* (BBC); *Crime 2* (BritBox); *The Woman in the Wall, Shetland, Granite Harbour, The Nest, EastEnders, Casualty, City Central, Low Winter Sun, Manhunters, Paradise Heights* (BBC); *Kin* (BRON Studios); *Blood* (West Road Pictures); *Dead Still* (Deadpan Pictures); *Jack Taylor* (Telegael); *Soldier Soldier* (ITV); *Trainspotting; Gregory's 2 Girls* (Channel 4 Films); *There You'll Find Me* (Sky) and *Silent Roar* (BBC Film).

Colin Campbell

Colin holds a BA in Acting from The Lir Academy at Trinity College Dublin, in partnership with RADA.

His stage credits include productions with the Abbey Theatre, Rough Magic, Landmark Productions, Hatch Theatre Company, Livin' Dred, the Corn Exchange, Soho Theatre, Irish Repertory Theatre and Theatre Gu Leòr, among others.

Roles include: Troshin in *Children of the Sun* (dir. Lynne Parker), Tom in *Colic* (dir. Annabelle Comyn), Karl in *Straight to Video* (dir. Phillip McMahon), the title role in *Tarry Flynn* (dir. Aaron Monaghan), Pig in *Disco Pigs* (dir. John Haidar), Jimmy in *Dublin by Lamplight* (dir. Annie Ryan), and Manus in *Through a Glass Darkly* (dir. Annie Ryan). Further work includes: *The Playboy of the Western World*, *The Jesus Trilogy*, *To the Lighthouse*, *Flights*, *Cuckoo*, *Scotties*, *Hotel 16*, *Council of Nicea*, *All That Is* and *The Windstealers*.

Colin was part of the Shakespeare's Globe Touring Ensemble, performing internationally in *Twelfth Night*, *The Comedy of Errors* and *Pericles*.

His screen work includes Channel 5's crime drama *Cooper and Fry*.

Seán Campion

Seán's recent screen work includes: the Bishop of Cork in *House of Guinness* (Netflix); Jimmy O'Dwyer in *Call the Midwife* (BBC); *The Mallorca Files* (Cosmopolitan Films/BBC Studios); the Chaplain in *Rillington Place* (BBC1); Will Harley in *Harley and the Davidsons* (Discovery Channel); and Byard Cary in Martin Campbell's feature film *The Foreigner*. Further credits include: *Mr Selfridge* (ITV); *United Passions*, *Borgia* (Atlantique); *Identity* (ITV); *Holby City* (BBC); *EastEnders* (BBC); and *Raw* (RTÉ).

On stage, Seán has worked extensively in Ireland and abroad. Highlights include: Older Daithí in *Once Before I Go* (Gate Theatre, dir. Selina Cartmell); Crazy Crow in *All the Angels* (Shakespeare's Globe, dir. Jonathan Munby); and Jake in *Stones in His Pockets* (Lyric Theatre, West End, Broadway), for which he was nominated for both an Olivier Award and a Tony Award. At the Abbey Theatre he has appeared in *Macbeth*, *The Silver Tassie*, *Observe the Sons of Ulster Marching Towards the Somme*, *King Lear*, *Sive* and *Big Maggie*, among others, with further stage work including: *Mutabilitie* and

Tarry Flynn (National Theatre); *Waiting for Godot* (Lyric Theatre); and *Miss Julie* (Everyman Palace).

Rhiannon May

Rhiannon is from Nottingham and the first deaf actor and BSL user to hold a regular role in a BBC series, starring as Cara Connelly in *Silent Witness* for four series. Her screen credits also include a leading role in *The Riley Sisters*, shown at the BFI London Film Festival, and an appearance in the BBC's LGBTQIA+ short film *Silent Pride*. On stage, Rhiannon has recently performed in *Antony and Cleopatra* at The Globe, the BBC Proms, and as the title role in *Alice in Wonderland* at Derby Theatre. She is a regular performer at *Night In Sign*, Fuse Theatre's deaf-led cabaret night.

Amy Molloy

Amy's theatre credits include: *The House* (Druid at Gaiety Theatre); *Akedah* (Hampstead Theatre, Best Lead Performance OFFIE nomination); *This is Paradise* (Traverse Theatre for Edinburgh Fringe, Critics Awards for Theatre in Scotland, Best Actress nomination); *Translations* (National Theatre); *Cotton Fingers* (Lustrum Award for Edinburgh Fringe at Summerhall and Irish/UK Tour); *Cyprus Avenue* (Royal Court Theatre/Public Theater NYC/Abbey Theatre Dublin, MAC Belfast); *Elizas Adventures in the Uncanny Valley* (Pan Pan at the Dublin Theatre Festival); *Into the Numbers* (Finborough); *Disco Pigs* (JMK Award, UK & Irish tour); *Playhouse Creatures* (Bruiser Theatre Co, Belfast); *Lieutenant of Inishmore* (CURVE); *Teaset* (Pleasance, Edinburgh Fringe); *Tejas Verdes* and *Villa* (Prime Cut, Belfast) and *John Gabriel Borkman* (Abbey Theatre and BAM Harvey NYC).

Her film credits include: *Chasing Millions*, *Love Without Walls*, *Animals*, *71*, *The Sea* and *Black Ice*. Her television credits include: *Say Nothing* (Disney/FX); *Spinster* (BBC Comedy);

Borderline (MGM plus/Prime UK); *Bloodlands*, *The Fall*, *Call the Midwife* and *Cyprus Avenue* (all BBC).

This production was funded by the Arts Council of Ireland Opera Projects and Production Award.

arts council an chomhairle ealaíon | funding opera

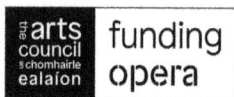

Her Father's Voice

Characters

Play

Carol, *thirties, a trainee doctor*
Frank, *thirties, Carol's husband, an opera composer*
Claudia, *fifties/sixties, Carol's mother*
Darragh, *fifties/sixties, Carol's father*
Marion, *twenties, Deaf*
Sarah, *six, Carol & Frank's daughter, Deaf*
Ciara, *six, Marion's daughter, Deaf*

Opera

Lifeguard, *twenties, Marion's boyfriend, Deaf*
Second Lifeguard
Graham, *a surgeon*
Audiologist
Children at the swimming pool

Notes on the script

/ indicates that the following line begins at this point.

– indicates that the character has an unspoken thought.

[words in brackets are not said aloud]

Text in bold italics is describing the action on film.

All dialogue within the film forms the libretto of the opera.

Signed lines don't need to be subtitled or interpreted for the audience.

** (double asterisk) denotes a slight jump forward in time.

Notes on the set

The play takes place in the contemporary extension at the rear of a large Victorian house in Dublin. The house faces a square with a residents' park in the centre. There is a study area off to one side that has a piano and a sofa bed. Within the extension is a modern, stylish kitchen and dining area. A door leads out to the garden, and another doorway leads to the hallway and front door. A third door is located in the study area that also leads to the main body of the house.

The opera takes place in another space, accompanied by the film footage. There is a sense that the opera has been implanted in the play.

Act One

Heavy rain. A light left on in the kitchen. **Carol** *and* **Frank** *are heard entering through the front door.*

Carol (*off*) Did you though?

Frank (*off*) Get inside you loon, you're shouting.

Carol *and* **Frank** *enter wearing soaked rain coats. Underneath are their fancy dinner party outfits.*

Carol I saw someone, Frank.

Frank Where?

Carol In the square.

Frank Just now?

Carol When we were getting out of the taxi, yeah.

Frank It's (*looks at the clock*) oh no, half past two in / the morning –

Carol A woman, I think.

Frank . . . very late for Mummy and Daddy to be / awake.

Carol In a blue coat. She was staring at us – Frank?

Frank A ghost maybe. Let's go to bed.

Carol I'm being serious.

Frank So am I. Ghosts are real.

Carol I'm gonna slap you. Maybe I should go out?

Frank Why?

Carol Because it's the right thing to do.

Frank I really don't think there is anyone there, love.

Carol Well, you wouldn't have seen her anyway. Too busy sulking.

Frank (*taking off his coat*)   Why would I be sulking?

Carol (*taking his coat, leaving the room*)   I dunno. You tell me.

Carol *exits.*

(*Off, shouting.*) Oh, I can't see anything from here – the trees are in the way. They're so big now. (*Coming back in*)   I spent my entire childhood staring out that window planning my escape. And here I am, back at square / one.

Frank   Car, you'll wake your mum and dad.

Carol   She looked at us, Frank.

Frank   What are you going to do?

Carol   I'll just / see if she

Frank   Run a medical assessment?

Carol   Oh shut up.

Frank (*playfully*)   Take her pulse? Are you at that / stage yet?

Carol   Don't be such a / dick.

Frank   Are you allowed to take a pulse?

Carol (*she runs after him to hit him, playfully*)   I actually am going to slap you now.

Frank (*laughing*)   Do no harm, doctor! Doctor! Do no harm!

She catches him, playfully slaps him, then they kiss.

Carol   I'm not a doctor yet.

Frank   Oh, in that case, do all the harm you want.

They kiss again.

Carol   I want a drink.

Frank   I want to sleep.

Carol   Let's have a drink.

Frank   No. Drinking is very bad for you.

Carol (*opening the drinks cupboard*)   A nightcap just.

Frank   What have they got?

Carol   Baileys. No. Gin. Oh, whiskey.

Frank   You naughty girl.

Carol   Would you like some of my daddy's whiskey?

Frank   I'm a bit scared of your daddy.

Carol   But what about his whiskey?

Frank   I'm not scared of his whiskey.

Carol   Grab two glasses then.

Frank *looks around completely lost.*

Frank   Where are the whiskey glasses?

Carol   Over there in the unit.

Frank   I have no idea where anything is.

Carol (*as she exits*)   Fill those. I'll just run up and check on Sarah.

Frank *fills the glasses, sits at the piano and picks out a melody. After a while,* **Carol** *enters.*

Carol   She's out cold – the little frog. (*Looks at the clock.*) Frank, look at the time.

Frank   Yeah, I know.

Carol   Six years old.

Frank *presses a final key.*

Frank   Why did you say I was a piano teacher?

Carol   When?

Frank   At dinner.

Carol   Because you are a piano teacher. (*About the whiskey.*) Is this mine?

Frank   Yes.

Carol   Are you not?

Frank   Oh. Okay.

Carol   What?

Frank   No, it's fine.

Carol   Are you not a piano teacher, though?

Frank   I'm a piano teacher for hire. I do not identify as a piano teacher.

Carol   Oh. (*Laughs.*) / Right

Frank   Don't laugh at me.

Carol   What do you identify as then?

Frank   You're slagging me now.

Carol   Sorry. I'm not.

Frank   I'm a composer, Car.

Carol   Yes, you are. You also are.

Frank   I've always been.

Carol   And a teacher, too. You're both.

Frank   You introduced me as 'a piano teacher to kiddies', I think you said.

Carol   Did I?

Frank   Yes.

Carol   Kiddies? Did I?

Frank   Were you trying to impress them?

Carol   Maybe, yeah. Cheers.

They toast.

To kiddies!

She laughs, he doesn't.

Sorry. To our beautiful daughter. Happy birthday, darling.

They drink.

Frank   Was the word occasional necessary?

Carol   What?

Frank   *Occasional* piano teacher to kiddies.

Carol   Probably not.

Frank   You may as well have said I'm your eunuch, stay at /
home husband who occasionally bangs spoons together with
some kiddies for fun.

Carol (*laughing*)   Eunuch! What? Oh come on, love. I just
told them what you do. That is what you do, isn't it?

Frank   It's what I've ended up doing.

Carol   But, it is what you do.

Frank   It's humiliating to have your wife pity you in her
introduction.

Carol   I don't pity you.

Frank   I heard pity.

Carol   You misheard then.

Frank   You made me sound like a child at the table / while
that . . .

Carol   I have no pity for you, Frank.

Frank   . . . asshole says, well it feels like pity, I felt
patronised and existentially challenged / when that . . .

Carol (*laughing*)   Existentially challenged! Okay. / Do you
want another drop?

Frank   . . . asshole belittles me about being a stay at home
dad. (*About the whiskey.*) No. What's his name, Graham?

Carol   Don't pretend you don't know his name.

Frank   Is it Graham?

Carol   Yes, Graham. He's going to be operating on our daughter. You've met him a thousand times.

Frank   I've met him once.

Carol   You know who Graham is.

Frank   'So you're the stay at home parent then, Frank?'

Carol   Women have to deal with that all the time.

Frank   Oh! Oh!!! (*Makes a klaxon sound.*) Stop everything! (*Makes whipping sounds.*) Mea culpa, mea culpa. I'm very grateful to have been privileged enough to be belittled about being a stay at home dad. Lucky me.

Carol *goes to top up* **Frank**'s *glass.*

I said no, we've got her swimming lessons / in (*looks at the clock*) oh Jesus, five hours, Car.

Carol   Just a drop, take the edge off. (*She fills the glass.*) Is there something wrong with being a piano teacher?

Frank   Of course not. (*About the whiskey.*) That's loads.

Carol   Are you ashamed of it?

Frank   You could have mentioned my commission.

Carol   Yes. I could have mentioned that. Mea culpa. (*Beat.*) Why didn't *you* mention it?

Frank   Only assholes volunteer celebratory information about themselves to strangers.

Carol   I've met a lot of those assholes.

Frank   That's your job.

Carol   What is?

Frank   'Frank is a composer, he has a commission actually'. And then I go 'oh . . . it's nothing really, just a short thing'. And then you say 'Stop being so modest darling, it's a big deal actually . . . blah blah blah'. That's how that works.

Carol   Noted.

Frank   What do you mean, noted? You know that's how it works. We used to do that kind of thing all the time.

Carol   Maybe I'm out of practice with talking bullshit.

Frank *scoffs.*

How's it going, anyway? Your commission?

Frank *drains his glass and stands up to go to bed.*

Oh, no. Sorry! Don't go! (*She clinks her glass, as if making a toast, and wanders towards* **Frank**.) Dearest assembled doctors of the hospital in which I am a lowly trainee on placement. This is my husband Frank, a gifted opera composer who is definitely not a eunuch. (*Going for his belt buckle.*) He has a delightful penis in fact –

Frank *steps away.*

You're really angry.

Frank   I'm not. (*Beat.*) Disappointed, maybe.

Carol   In *me?*

Frank   I felt humiliated.

Carol   By me?

Frank   By them.

Carol   Okay.

Frank   And by you. Yeah.

Carol   Well, honestly, Frank, you're a big boy. You could have just told them you were a composer.

Frank   I did.

Carol   What?

Frank   Later. When I was talking to Graham. Just the two of us.

Carol   Then what are you so pissed off about?

Frank   When you introduced me . . . your voice . . . I heard this kind of pity / and –

Carol   I do not pity you, Frank.

Frank   And guilt.

Carol   Sorry?

Frank   I heard guilt too.

Carol   Guilt?

I am not guilty.

Frank   –

Carol   I have nothing to feel guilty about.

Frank   –

Carol   Frank?

Frank   Ok.

Carol   Frank?

Frank   I said ok.

Beat.

Carol   I'm sorry / if . . .

Frank   It's fine.

Carol   . . . I upset you. I don't want you to / be upset.

Frank   I know that.

Carol   I never want to upset you.

Frank   I know. (*Beat.*) They're just not our kind of people.

Carol   Doctors? Well, I'm going to be one at some stage. Fingers crossed.

Frank   I mean – you know what I mean.

Carol   I don't.

Frank   They think they're . . . better than us. Than me, actually.

Carol   Do they?

Frank   When I told Graham that I was a composer, he asked me what I was working on.

Carol   Which is nice, showing an interest.

Frank   I told him about my commission. He asked me what it's about.

Carol   Okay.

Frank   I don't know what it's about. Do I?

Carol   That's okay too.

Frank   No, it's not. Not when I'm sat in front of doctor big balls and / I've already had to try and fight for some kind . . .

Carol   / Eunuchs and big balls. I'm sensing a theme.

Frank   . . . of status or . . . then a question like that . . . 'what's it about Frank' . . . I felt so . . .

Carol   He was just asking you a question.

Frank (*strained*)   Yes.

Carol   What did you say to him then?

Frank   I . . . (*remembering it, mortified*) oh, made up some . . . shite. A chamber piece about . . . war, I think I said. Lots of percussion. Violins . . . might have mentioned castanets.

Carol (*laughing*)   Did you actually say the word castanets? To Graham?

Frank (*impersonating* **Graham**)   'I think your ambitions with this opera are impressive, Frank, but lots of percussion in an opera about war? Sounds a little on the nose don't you think.'

Carol (*laughing*)   Oh no. What did you say then?

Frank   Nothing. Thank you, or something. Then I hid in the bathroom for a bit.

Carol   Maybe you *should* write something about war?

Frank   Ding ding! I'm done.

Carol   What? It's not a bad idea.

Frank   Let's go to bed.

Carol   Did you ask him your question? About the implant.

Frank   Of course I didn't.

Carol   What?

Frank   –

Carol   That was the whole point of the night Frank.

Frank   I didn't want to be laughed at.

Carol   I don't think he'd have laughed.

Frank   I don't like him, Car, okay.

Carol   He's not what you'd call a charmer, Graham, but – and this is going to piss you off – it's a big deal that we got that time with him tonight. Most parents don't get any time at all with the surgeon. So . . . it's a bit of a pity that you didn't ask him about the music thing. I know / it's important

Frank   The music thing?

Carol   You know what I mean.

Frank   Okay.

Carol   And, just to say – I put myself out, wangling an invitation to that dinner party with doctors from work. So . . . you know . . .

Frank   Are you trying to make me feel bad?

Carol   No, I'm trying to help you understand the rarity of what we've just had. That's all.

Frank   He's an asshole, Carol.

Carol   Yes.

Frank   And the thought of him boring a hole into our happy little daughter's skull –

Carol   He's an excellent surgeon, Frank. The best.

Frank   I don't like him.

Carol   You don't have to like him, you just have to trust him.

Claudia *enters in her pajamas.*

Claudia   There's someone out in the square.

Carol (*to* **Frank**)   I told you!

Claudia   Your father is very upset by it.

Frank   Did we wake you?

Claudia   Of course you did, like jackals down here the pair of you.

Frank   Sorry, Claudia.

Claudia   She's just standing out there. It's awful.

Carol   It's a woman isn't it?

Claudia   A child in the rain like that. Where's my phone?

Frank   A child?

Claudia   She has a child with her.

Carol   Jesus.

Claudia   I'm going to call the guards.

Carol   The guards? / Mum?

Frank   Don't do that. I'll go out and / see what

Carol   Oh, now you want to go out?

Claudia   Do not. She could be on drugs or / something.

Frank   On drugs?

Carol   I should have just gone over when we got out of / the taxi.

Frank   What makes you think she's on drugs?

Claudia   Did you move my phone, Carol?

Carol   No, Mum.

Claudia   Why are you both down here in the pitch darkness?

Carol   It's not pitch darkness.

Claudia   Are you drunk?

Carol   A little bit.

Frank   I really don't think we need to / call the guards.

Claudia   Will one of you put on the big light?

Frank   She's not harming anyone.

Claudia   Darragh is very upset, Frank. She's upsetting my husband.

A knock at the door. Silence.

Carol   I'll just –

Claudia   Don't open it, Car.

Another knock, a little harder this time.

Call the guards, one of you.

Frank   Or we could just open the door?

The doorbell rings.

**

Marion, *wearing an electric blue coat, stands in the living room soaking wet.* **Frank** *and* **Claudia** *are looking at her.* **Ciara**, *exhausted, holds on to her mother.*

Marion (*signs to* **Frank**)   I didn't know where to go, sorry.

Claudia   What is she saying?

Frank   She's sorry. (*Signs.*) It's / okay.

Carol (*entering with a towel*)   Here you are, you poor thing.

Marion *looks at* **Ciara**.

Is she alright?

Marion   Yes.

Carol   She's soaked.

Marion (*signs to* **Frank**)   It's so / late. I –

Carol   Here, give me your coat.

Frank (*signs*)   She wants your coat.

Marion (*signs to* **Frank**)   I feel stupid . . . I had nowhere else / to

Carol   Do you want me to run up and / get a hairdryer?

Frank (*signs*)   What happened?

Marion (*signs to* **Frank**)   If I had your phone number, I would have texted.

Claudia   I'm Claudia. I'm Carol's mother.

Marion   I'm sorry, it's so late.

Claudia   We got a bit of a fright.

Marion (*signs to* **Frank**)   I had a . . . fight with my boyfriend. He was so – (*she checks* **Ciara**)

Claudia   Car, I'm in my pajamas.

Frank   She had a fight with her boyfriend, she said.

Claudia   A fight?

Marion *picks* **Ciara** *up.*

Carol   Are you alright?

Marion (*signs*)   Is Darragh here?

Claudia   What did she say?

Frank   She's asking for Darragh.

Claudia   Darragh? Why?

Marion   I need to talk to him.

Act Two

Scene One

The following morning. **Darragh**, *wearing a rain coat, is drinking coffee. There are some mucky gardening gloves set aside.* **Marion's** *things are scattered across the sofa bed.* **Claudia** *enters in a dressing gown.*

Claudia (*surprised*)   Are they gone?

Darragh   Ages ago, yeah.

Claudia   Are they? What time is it?

She looks at the clock.

Darragh   They went an hour or two ago, I'd say.

Claudia   Why didn't they wake me?

Darragh   Maybe they felt bad.

Claudia   How come you didn't go?

Darragh   I didn't want to.

Claudia   Oh?

Darragh   She had a head on her this morning. They both did.

Claudia   They were drinking / whiskey.

Darragh   Let them go on their own, I thought.

Claudia   Did you see Marion this morning?

Darragh   Who?

Claudia   The Deaf girl who came in the night.

Darragh   Oh.

Claudia   She slept down here. You didn't come across her?

Darragh   Whose whiskey?

Claudia (*looking at the clock again*)   It's too late to follow on now. Ah, I really wanted to see her swim on her birthday.

Silence.

Doesn't matter. (*Beat.*) Were you in the garden?

Darragh   Yeah.

Claudia   In that rain?

Darragh   I had my coat.

Darragh *goes to the drinks cupboard.*

Claudia   Have you seen my phone?

Darragh   Look Claud.

Claudia   What?

Darragh   Half the bottle they drank.

Claudia   They were fairly polluted alright.

Darragh   When are they going back to their own house?

Claudia   They can't afford to rent their own house anymore, Dar.

Darragh   A student, in her thirties.

Claudia   Ah, will you stop.

Darragh   And what's he?

Claudia   Doing his best, stop I said.

Darragh   And little Sarah –

Claudia   Stop.

Darragh   Freeloaders and whiskey thieves.

Claudia   They are here now. They'll go again. We should cherish it.

Darragh   Grown adults, is all I'm saying.

Claudia (*finding her phone*)   Ah. (*Checks it.*) No one wants me. Would you like another coffee?

Darragh   See how they're getting on.

Claudia   What?

Darragh   Phone Carol.

Claudia   Will I? (*Dialing.*) Okay.

Darragh   Tell her I have a present for Sarah.

Claudia   I bought her one from the two of us.

Darragh   Well I have one from just me.

Claudia   Do you? What is it? (**Carol** *answers the phone.*) Hi Car. / Where are you?

Darragh   It's a surprise.

Claudia   A surprise? (*To* **Carol**.) I'm talking to your father. You left without me. Why didn't you wake me? Ah. You got / a cake?

Darragh   Did the Deaf girl go?

Claudia   Marion is her name. She's at the pool with them. (*To* **Carol**.) I'm talking to your father again. What kind of / a cake?

Darragh   Ask her if . . .

Claudia (*to* **Carol**)   Iron Man. What's that?

Darragh   . . . if she's coming back with them?

Claudia   Who? (*To* **Carol**.) Your father / is asking me something.

Darragh   Marion.

Claudia   Her things are here, so I assume she is.

Darragh *stands and wanders over to look at* **Marion**'s *things.*

Darragh   She's got a lot of gear with her.

Claudia (*to* **Carol**)   Will you take photos?

Darragh   Why did she bring all this stuff?

Claudia (*to* **Carol**)   He's filming at the pool? Is that not a bit weird? (*To* **Darragh**.) Don't touch her things, Dar. (*To* **Carol**.) I know, I know . . . it's just that / it's a public pool.

Darragh   Is she moving in?

Claudia   Okay, alright, alright. See you in a bit then.

Claudia *hangs up.*

Frank offered her and her child a bed for the night, that's all.

Darragh   Frank did?

Darragh *pokes at* **Marion**'*s things.*

Claudia   Dar, I asked you not to touch her things. (*Beat.*) They did a cake for Sarah at the pool.

Darragh   So.

Claudia   I made a cake for her.

Darragh   She can have two cakes.

Claudia   Yeah, I know.

Darragh   Can't she?

Claudia   Of course she can, yeah –

Beat.

I bought some decorations. . . but there is a party at the pool now –

Beat.

Doesn't matter.

Beat.

She asked for you.

Darragh   Who did?

Claudia   Marion. Last night, when she came in.

Darragh   Oh? What did she say, exactly?

Claudia   That she wanted to talk to you.

Darragh   About what?

Claudia   She didn't say. I told her you were asleep.

They sit in a silence for a bit.

Claudia   Do you want another coffee?

Darragh   No. I'll be awake all night.

Claudia   It's still early, you'll be alright.

Darragh   No thanks, Claud.

Claudia   How do you know her?

Darragh   From the school, whenever I pick Sarah up from school. Marion's daughter is in Sarah's class so –

Claudia   What do you talk about?

Darragh   I just say hello.

Claudia   And that's it?

Darragh   I suppose so, yeah.

Claudia   Do you have any idea why she might arrive here in the middle of the night and ask for you then?

Darragh   I don't know

Claudia   To say hello back, is it?

Darragh   Don't be smart.

Claudia   Is it Louise?

Darragh   –

Claudia   Something to do with Louise, maybe?

Darragh   What do you mean?

Claudia   Is that why she wants to talk to you, maybe?

Darragh   Might, em – yeah.

Beat.

I asked Marion if –

Claudia   If?

Darragh   Anyone she knew might –

Claudia   Know her, is it?

Darragh   Louise, yeah. Or know something about –

Claudia   Where she is?

Darragh   Yeah.

Claudia   Or how she's doing, is it?

Darragh   Anything. Yeah. At all.

Claudia   To find out for you? Within the . . . community, like.

Darragh   Yes.

Claudia   When did you ask her to do that?

Darragh   What does it matter when?

Claudia   Well, was it recently?

Darragh   Just em . . . what is it today?

Claudia   Sunday.

Darragh   Last Thursday. No. I was at the doctor Thursday. Friday maybe, then.

Claudia   Friday.

Darragh   Yeah. When I collected Sarah from school on Friday.

Claudia   And what made you ask that?

Beat.

Has something happened, Dar?

Darragh   What do you mean?

Claudia   You're not sleeping.

Darragh   –

Claudia   For months you're not. Since Carol came home, really.

Beat.

What has you thinking about Louise?

Darragh   I'm always [thinking about Louise].

Claudia   Are you?

Darragh   Yes.

Claudia   You never say anything to me.

Darragh   She's my sister, Claud.

Claudia   I know that love.

Darragh   And the doctor said I have / to –

Claudia   Is *that* what this is?

Darragh   . . . for my heart, he said.

Claudia   Ah, Dar, he said there's nothing to worry about really.

Darragh   No.

Claudia   It's a small thing, in and out.

Darragh   Still.

Claudia   Is that what has you like / this?

Darragh   So . . . of course I'm thinking about her.

Claudia   Your heart is / fine.

Darragh   My only sister, Claud.

Claudia   I know.

Darragh   All I have.

Claudia   You have us, love.

The sound of the rain.

Darragh   That hasn't stopped since . . .

Claudia   No, it's desperate.

Darragh   Was she soaked?

Claudia   Marion? Car brought down the hairdryer.

Darragh   A child out in that.

The rain.

Claudia   How long have you been thinking about Louise?

Darragh   Go on then, I will have a coffee.

Claudia *gets up to make the coffee.*

I think I know what –

Claudia   What?

Darragh   What Marion wants to tell me. I think she'll tell me that Louise is dead.

Claudia *stops.*

Claudia   Oh, Dar.

Darragh   I have a feeling.

Claudia   No. You're being morbid.

Darragh   Why would she ask for me? In the night, like that.

Claudia   She came in the night because she had a row with her boyfriend.

Darragh   I couldn't cope / if –

Claudia   Honestly love, there's no reason to / think

Darragh   I wouldn't be able for it Claud.

The hall door opens.

Carol (*off*)   Hello! Hello!

Claudia   Oh, hello?

Carol (*off*)   Frank can you get her to –

Claudia   They were quick.

Darragh *stands, takes his gardening gloves and goes out the back door to the garden.*

Where are you going?

Marion *and* **Carol** *are in the hallway with* **Ciara** *and* **Sarah**.

Carol (*off*)   Sarah, stop it. Just take it / off love

Frank (*off*)   Let her wear it if she wants to wear it.

Carol (*off to* **Sarah**)   Love, you need to take this / off.

Carol *enters with* **Sarah** *who is still in her swimsuit and goggles, and a dry-robe.*

Claudia   There's the birthday girl! (*About the goggles.*) What are you doing with those on your face?

Carol *tries to take the goggles off.*

Carol (**Sarah** *slaps her*)   Ow. Sarah!

Claudia   Have you got a kiss for Granny?

Sarah *leaves.*

No kiss then.

Carol   Sorry, Mum.

Carol *goes to the fridge.* **Marion** *enters with* **Ciara**.

Claudia   Oh Marion! (*Looking at her pajamas.*) I do wear clothes, I swear!

Marion (*signs to* **Ciara**)   Go and play with Sarah.

Ciara *runs out.*

Claudia   She's a lovely girl.

Marion   Thanks.

An awkward moment.

I'll just check my phone.

Marion *goes over to the study area.*

Carol   She's so mean to me.

Claudia   Who?

Carol   Sarah.

Claudia   She's six years old, Carol.

Carol   Are there any of her yoghurts?

Claudia   In the bottom of the fridge. How was the party?

Carol   It wasn't really a party. We just asked the lifeguard to make a bit of a fuss of her and – (*seeing the cake in the fridge*) did you make a cake, Mum?

Claudia   Yes. I didn't realise you were bringing your own cake to the pool.

Carol   Oh. Frank wanted to have something with the Deaf children, her pals. It was a last-minute thing.

Carol *takes a yoghurt from the fridge.*

Claudia   Right.

Carol   Mum, that's so nice that you –

Carol *starts looking around.*

Claudia   What are you looking for now?

Carol   Paracetamol.

Claudia   There, in the drawer. Would the other children not have come here?

Carol   From the pool?

Claudia   Yeah, for a party.

Carol   Oh . . . it's your house, Mum. I'd feel bad.

Claudia (*laughs*)   Oh!

Carol   What?

Claudia   You're terribly worried about putting us out, are you?

Carol   I am very respectful.

Claudia   You drank half of your father's whiskey last night.

Carol (*taking the paracetamol*)   Did we?

Frank *enters with the Iron Man cake in one hand, and his tripod for the phone in the other.*

Frank (*putting down the tripod*)   Is that paracetamol?

Carol (*indicating the packet*)   There.

Claudia   I heard she had cake by the pool.

Frank   No one ate cake in the pool, that was just for photos.

Claudia   I don't understand that.

Frank   A couple of them had a slice after. (*About the cake.*) Can I put this in the fridge?

Claudia (*about the cake*)   Give it to me here.

Frank *gives* **Claudia** *the cake. He plays the footage from the pool on his phone. We hear the sound of the pool and* **Frank** *and* **Carol** *talking.* **Claudia** *watches over his shoulder.*

Claudia   Ah stop. Look –

Carol *hands a glass of water to* **Frank**. *He gives the phone to* **Claudia**, *then takes the paracetamol.*

Frank   They're all so clumsy looking, like little drunks – which is adorable, obviously.

Carol   Maybe we can lower the volume on that a little?

Frank   Just the button at the top Claudia.

Claudia   I know how phones work.

Carol   Just turn the sound off. It's mainly me and Frank talking shite.

Claudia *turns the sound on the phone off.*

Claudia   I suppose this is what it's like for Sarah all the time.

Frank   What?

Claudia   Like this, with the sound off. (*Beat.*) Ah, they're gorgeous. It would have been nice to ask those children here for a party, no?

Frank   Mm. Carol?

Carol   You have to give people notice.

Frank   No you don't.

Carol   Frank / don't

Claudia   Why didn't you then?

Carol   Because she has her surgery tomorrow / and

Frank   Carol isn't super comfortable with the Deaf mums.

Claudia   Oh? Aren't you?

Frank   She feels left out with the sign language. Right love?

Carol   Okay, Frank.

Frank   What?

Carol   Just leave it, okay?

Carol *goes out with the yoghurt for* **Sarah**.

Claudia (*watching the footage*)   Are you two fighting?

Frank   No, we're just hungover.

Frank *watches the footage with* **Claudia** *for a moment.*

Claudia   You've got a lot of footage of the lifeguard.

Frank *takes the phone and goes to the study area.*

Where are you going with that? I want to see her blow / out the candles.

Frank   Just want to jot something down, Claudia. Sorry.

Frank *sits at the piano near where* **Marion** *is sitting. He places the phone in front of him, footage still running, and plays a little.* **Claudia** *takes the Iron Man cake in the back kitchen, and dumps it.*

Marion (*signs*)   My phone died.

Frank (*signs*)   I'm sure we have a charger.

Claudia (*re-entering*)   Would anyone like a coffee?

Frank (*signs*)   Would you like a coffee?

Marion (*signs*)   I would actually, yeah.

Frank   Marion would.

Claudia   I was making one for Dar but he's gone out to the garden.

Claudia *prepares coffee for* **Marion**. *She watches* **Frank** *and* **Marion** *signing.*

Marion (*signs*)   I feel a bit awkward.

Frank (*signs*)   Why?

Marion (*signs*)   I have to speak to Darragh.

Frank (*signs*)   About what?

Marion (*signs*)   About his sister. She's dead.

Carol *enters*.

Carol   Are you making coffee?

Claudia   I am.

Frank (*signs*)   His sister?

Marion (*signs*)   Yeah, he asked me to find out about her.

Carol (*baby voice*)   Will you make one for me, Mommy?

Frank (*signs*)   I didn't know he had a sister.

Claudia   You crack me up when you do that voice.

Marion (*signs*)   You didn't know about her?

Frank (*signs*)   No, this is the first I've heard.

Carol *looks over at* **Frank** *and* **Marion**.

Marion (*signs*)   They were estranged. Her name was Louise, she was Deaf.

Frank (*signs*)   I've never heard of her. Louise.

Claudia *finishes making a coffee*.

Carol   Thanks.

Claudia   No. This one is for Marion.

Marion (*signs*)   I don't know how to tell Darragh?

Carol   Oh. What are these?

Claudia   Decorations.

Frank (*signs*)   When / did she die?

Carol   For what?

Marion (*signs*)   A few years ago.

Claudia   For a party, for Sarah.

Carol   I didn't know we were having a party.

Claudia   Well, I thought I'd put them up around the place this morning and surprise her, but . . . doesn't matter.

Frank (*signs*)   Carol never said she had an aunt.

Marion (*signs*)   Maybe she doesn't want you to know.

Carol   Oh Mum, I feel bad now.

Frank (*signs*)   What do you mean?

Claudia   Oh do you? Give this to Marion and I'll make your one. Wait (*to* **Frank**) milk for the coffee Frank?

Frank (*signs*)   Do you want milk?

Marion (*signs*)   Yes. Small bit.

Frank   A small drop.

Claudia   Pour some milk in it, Car, will you?

Carol *goes to the fridge.*

Frank (*signs*)   Do you want me to tell Darragh for you?

Marion (*signs*)   No, he asked me to keep it private. It's just . . . what if he's angry with me?

Frank (*signs*)   Why would he be angry?

Marion (*signs*)   It's not a very nice story.

Frank (*signs*)   If he asked you to find out, then you're just doing what he asked. It's nothing to do with you.

Carol *brings the coffee to* **Marion**.

Claudia (*from across the kitchen*)   You've gotten very good at sign language, Frank.

Marion (*signs*)   Please / don't say anything.

Frank   Oh, trying my best is all. (*Signs.*) I won't.

Claudia   None of us know a word of it. Isn't that / shameful.

Carol That's not true. (*Signs.*) Thank you. That's thank you, right?

Marion Yes. (*Signs, receiving the coffee.*) Thank you.

Beat. **Frank** *and* **Marion** *are behaving a little strangely.*

Carol (*to* **Frank**) Is everything okay?

Frank Yeah.

Claudia Frank, Rita phoned yesterday evening.

Frank Sorry, who?

Claudia Rita, she's the house directly across the square. She wondered would you do a piano lesson on Wednesday afternoons with her grandson? I said you're always here on a Wednesday / afternoon.

Carol Mum, Frank is a composer. He's got to focus on / his own –

Frank Rita, did you say?

Claudia Yes. An older lady. Here since the year dot.

Carol A curtain twitcher.

Claudia I didn't know what price to tell her, but you can hash that out.

Frank Oh.

Claudia A premium price now, Frank, she's loaded.

Frank Right. I'll add a zero so.

Claudia Do. (*Beat.*) Will you go out and check on Darragh for me love? He's out in that rain all morning.

Carol I'll go.

Frank No, I'll do it. It's fine.

Frank *exits out the back door. An awkward moment, the women are not sure how to progress.*

Marion   This is a beautiful house.

Claudia   It's Darragh's family home. We inherited it.

Another awkward pause.

His mother and father . . . spoiled him rotten.

Carol   Have you heard from your boyfriend?

Marion   No.

Carol   But he saw you this morning. With us.

Claudia   You saw him?

Carol   Marion's boyfriend is the lifeguard at the pool.

Claudia   The one who did the birthday cake?

Marion   Yes.

Claudia   He's very handsome.

Marion   He's an asshole.

Claudia   Oh?

Marion   We fight a lot.

Claudia   Do you and your daughter live with him?

Marion   Yes. At his mother's house. I've lived there for almost a year now.

Claudia   Where were you before?

Marion   The UK. I'm from England.

Ciara *comes into the kitchen, snuggles into* **Marion**.

Marion (*signs*)   Okay?

Ciara (*signs*)   Toilet?

Carol   Is she alright?

Marion   She just wants to go to the toilet.

Claudia   In the hall. There's one under the stairs.

Marion (*signs*)   In the hall, under the stairs.

Ciara *doesn't leave, she holds on to* **Marion**.

Marion   Go on then.

Marion *kisses her on the forehead.* **Ciara** *begins to leave.*

(*Waves for her attention.*) Wash your hands when you're finished please.

Ciara *exits.*

Marion   She's not always like that . . . just, we had a rough night.

Carol   She's very sweet with you.

Marion   Frank told me that you've been struggling, a bit, with Sarah.

Carol   Did he?

Marion   Sorry, was I not supposed to say that?

Claudia   I think it's Frank who wasn't supposed to say that.

Marion   Oh.

Claudia   She's / not struggling

Carol   It's okay, Mum. Sarah's more of a Daddy's girl.

Claudia   At the moment, just. Things change.

Carol   I'm not here a lot because of the hours in the hospital / and that . . .

Marion   Do you think it's because she's Deaf?

Claudia   Not at all.

Marion   It's ok to say yes, I won't get offended.

Carol   Yes. I do, a bit. Yeah. Which is why the implant is . . . so important.

Marion   When is the surgery?

Carol   Monday.

Marion   You mean tomorrow?

Carol   Yes. (*A breath.*) Tomorrow.

Claudia   We're all a bit apprehensive. It's okay, love.

Marion (*signs*)   Happy Birthday.

Carol   Sorry, I don't understand.

Marion   It's Happy Birthday. (*Signs.*) Happy Birthday. You can sign it for Sarah later, she'll like that.

Carol   Oh. (*Signs.*) Happy Birthday?

Marion   Yes, like that.

Carol   Thanks.

Marion   Why did you wait so long to get the implant? People usually do it when the child is a baby.

Carol   Oh. A million reasons, we tried hearing aids and all that . . . but, mainly Frank. He's been . . . worried about everything that can go wrong / surgery

Claudia   Nothing will go / wrong.

Carol   Then, last night –

Claudia   What?

Carol   I arranged for us to have dinner with the surgeon, for Frank to ask a question he's been wanting to ask. It's awkward, the surgeon happens to be a boss of mine . . .

Marion   No way.

Carol   Yes. I'm on placement – trying to become a doctor. And, it didn't go super well. Frank just didn't . . .

Claudia   What did he want to ask about?

Carol   The surgery, risks and . . . I dunno, if she'll hear music.

Claudia   What kind of a thing is that to be worried about?

Carol   It's important to him, Mum.

Marion   I feel bad. I think I'm the one who has made him worried.

Claudia   Really?

Marion   We talk about the surgery sometimes, when the girls are swimming. I was just giving him a Deaf perspective on it.

Carol   Oh.

Claudia   What did you say to him?

Marion   I didn't try to stop him or anything, we were just talking. I just told him my opinion.

Claudia   Oh. That's a pity.

Carol   Are you against them?

Marion   Implants? No.

Claudia   So what did you say to him then?

Marion   Just I know a guy who had a bad experience, that's all. It didn't work, and he still gets a lot of pain.

Carol   Oh.

Marion   I didn't mean to make him worry.

Beat.

Claudia   Well, maybe you could say something else to him then.

Marion   Me?

Claudia   Yeah. Say something positive, maybe.

Marion   Like what?

Claudia   Like you think it is going to be okay.

Marion   I'm not a doctor.

Claudia   You could reassure him. For us. We would be very grateful.

Marion   I don't know what I would say.

Claudia   I'm sure you'll think of something.

Carol   I do think it would help. Coming from you.

Marion   Okay.

Carol   Will you?

Marion   Yeah, okay.

Carol *gives her a kiss on the cheek.* **Marion** *stands up, like she's looking for something.*

Carol   Do you need something?

Marion   Frank said he'd get a charger for my phone. It died.

Carol   Oh? Which phone is it?

Marion *shows her the phone.*

I've got the same one. One sec.

Carol *leaves the room.* **Claudia** *goes to* **Marion**.

Claudia   What did you and your boyfriend fight about? Do you mind me asking?

Marion   –

Claudia   Was he violent?

Marion   He called me a slut and he – em – spat in my face.

Claudia   Spat at you?

Marion   In front of Ciara, yes.

Claudia   Is he Ciara's father?

Marion   Sorry?

Claudia   Is the lifeguard Ciara's father?

Marion   Oh, no. He's another asshole.

Claudia   That's disgusting that he spat at you.

Marion   He has a bad temper. I'm the same. We do things to hurt each other.

Claudia   To hurt each other.

Marion   Sometimes, yeah.

Claudia   Right. (*Beat.*) What will you do now?

Carol *re-enters with the charger.*

Carol   Is it this one?

Marion   Yes.

Claudia   Marion was just telling me about last night. Her boyfriend spat at her.

Carol   What?

Marion   We were having an argument about . . . em, boundaries.

Carol   And he spat at you?

Marion   He's been asking me to do things that . . . I didn't mind doing at the start, but now I feel uncomfortable.

Claudia   Oh?

Marion   Stuff he's seeing on porn, I think. He's been choking me, and grabbing my hair –

Claudia   The lifeguard?

Carol   This is not where I thought this was going.

Marion   Is it okay to say all of this?

Carol   Say whatever you like.

Marion   Then he acts like golden boy in front of everyone else. His mother thinks he's an angel.

Carol   I get the impression we don't like the mother.

Claudia   No.

Marion   I don't want Ciara to see him treat me like that. It's –

Carol   Horrible.

Marion   Anyway . . . I shouldn't have come here.

Carol   Come here?

Claudia   What's that got to do with it?

Carol   You were right to / come here.

Marion   Nothing. Just – it's a very small community. Everyone knows everyone's business. And, like I said, everyone loves him. (*Beat.*) And I'm English too, so . . . I'm completely fucked.

Marion *is a bit overwhelmed.*

I know a girl in Sligo. A Deaf girl. She's nice.

Carol   Sligo?

Marion   Yeah. I'll text her, see if we can go there for a while.

Claudia   That sounds like a good idea.

Marion   I just need to charge my phone.

Carol   Oh. Right, yes. (*Handing her the charger.*) Here. (*Beat.*) Do you need anything else?

Marion   Would it be okay if I used your shower?

Carol   Of course. / It's upstairs.

Carol *and* **Marion** *exit.*

Claudia   The guest towels are on the left in the hot press, Car.

Claudia *is alone. She looks at the clock.* **Frank** *and* **Darragh** *enter.*

Frank   Found this fella digging a hole.

Claudia   A hole? (*About his mucky shoes.*) Your shoes, Dar.

Frank   In your flower beds, yeah.

Claudia   What were you digging a hole for, Dar?

Frank   Were you trying to escape?

Darragh   From what?

Frank   It was just a / joke.

Claudia   Is that what you were / doing –

Darragh   Ah, leave me alone. Just something I'd buried, that's all –

Claudia   You buried?

Darragh   A biscuit box, green. When I was young.

Claudia   Are you going mad, Dar?

Darragh   No, I am not going mad. Stop it.

Claudia   A box?

Darragh   I'm not going mad, stop saying that.

Claudia   I only said it once.

Darragh   I can dig holes in my own garden, can't I? (*To* **Frank**.) Or do I need your permission now?

Frank   What?

Darragh   Where is your house guest?

Frank   My –

Claudia   She's gone up for a shower.

Frank   Sorry, have I done something wrong?

Claudia   Do you want your coffee now, Dar?

Darragh   Is she going to leave?

Claudia   She's texted a friend in Sligo, a girl she knows.

Frank   In Sligo?

Claudia   Yeah, she thinks she can stay there for a bit.

Darragh   Go on then, Claud.

Claudia   What?

Darragh   I'll chance a coffee. Where is the birthday girl?

Claudia   In the front room.

Darragh   And some biscuits, maybe.

Darragh *leaves the kitchen.*

Frank   I think I upset him.

Claudia   No, he's just tired. (*Making the coffee.*) Did Marion tell you what she wants to speak to Darragh about?

Frank   Hm?

Claudia   Earlier, when you were signing with her?

Frank   Oh. No.

Claudia   Okay. You might give her a lift to the train station. When she's finished with her shower.

Frank   Yeah, no bother.

Claudia *takes the coffee and biscuits and exits.* **Marion***'s phone dings.* **Carol** *enters.*

Carol   Marion needs the hairdryer for Ciara's hair.

Frank   So, your dad has a sister called Louise.

Carol   What?

Frank   Marion told me. And that she's Deaf, Louise.

Carol   Yes, I know that.

Frank   You never said anything.

Carol   Well, I've never met her. Dad doesn't talk about her.

Frank   How come?

Carol   How does Marion know about / her?

Frank   Why don't you talk about her?

Carol   I don't know all the details about your aunts and uncles, do I?

Frank   I don't have any Deaf family members.

Carol   Is that what you were both talking about earlier? When you were / signing?

Frank   Why don't I know about her?

Carol   What's she doing? Sticking her fucking oar in.

Frank   She found out about Louise because your dad asked her to.

Carol   He asked her to?

Frank   That's what she said, yes.

Beat.

So, Sarah has a family member who is Deaf.

Carol   Yeah.

Frank   Had.

Carol   What?

Frank   She died. Marion said.

Carol   Oh. Jesus. Oh. That's . . . very sad.

Frank   That's what Marion needs to tell your dad.

Carol   Oh.

Beat.

Frank   I'm sorry.

Carol   For what?

Frank   Your aunt.

Carol   Oh, em. I mean I never . . . thanks. It's just, I never met the woman – shit, this is – poor Dad.

Frank   –

Carol   Em. (*Beat.*) Marion said that you told her I'm struggling with Sarah.

Frank   What? No, I only said / that

Carol   It's okay, I just –

Frank   I didn't say struggle, I / was more talking about –

Carol   It's fine, it's the truth. I just didn't think that you . . . em –

They are at a loss.

What was I doing?

Frank   The hairdryer. It's okay, I'll go.

Frank *takes the hairdryer and exits.* **Carol** *is alone on stage.* **Sarah** *enters, still in her goggles.*

Carol   Hello little frog, you've got to take those off love. Come, let Mummy do it.

Sarah *doesn't come.*

(*Signs.*) Happy Birthday. Happy Birthday.

Sarah *doesn't react.*

Mummy would really love a cuddle, little frog.

Sarah *doesn't.*

No? Then Mummy will just have to cuddle you against your will.

Carol *cuddles* **Sarah**, *who squirms.* **Carol** *holds on tighter. It's unsettling.* **Sarah** *screams, and* **Carol** *releases her with a jolt.* **Sarah** *runs off.*

Okay. Fine. Go away then. Jesus. Go.

Carol *is alone.* **Marion's** *phone dings in the study.* **Darragh** *is in the doorway, holding his coffee.*

Darragh   Are we doing a cake, then?

Carol   In a bit, I think.

Darragh   Your mum made a cake especially.

Carol   I know.

Beat.

Darragh   And I have a present for her.

Carol   That's nice of you.

Carol *opens a bag of birthday decorations.*

Darragh   When will I give it to her?

Carol   Whenever you like, Dad.

Frank *enters the study area through another door, sits at his piano, plays the footage on his phone and starts to pick out a tune.*

Have you spoken to Marion?

Darragh   No. (*Beat.*) Why?

Carol   She's leaving soon. Going to Sligo I think.

Darragh   Your mother said, yeah.

The sound of the rain and the piano.

She really wanted to go with you this morning.

Carol   Who?

Darragh   Your mother. She likes to watch her swim.

Carol   Then she can watch her next weekend.

Darragh   She won't be swimming next weekend.

Carol   No. You're right. She won't.

Darragh   It means a lot to your mother, being included.

Carol   Okay Dad.

Darragh   Today will be the last time she swims for a long time.

Carol   Not 'a long time', don't be so dramatic! For a couple of weeks, maybe. Jesus. Everyone just needs to calm down.

Claudia *enters, dressed up.*

Claudia (*looking at the clock*)   We'd want to get started if we're doing a cake and that.

Carol   Okay, I'll do it now. (*Seeing* **Claudia**.) You're all dressed up, Mum.

Claudia   Am I? What can I do?

Carol (*taking balloons from the bag*)   Will you blow up some of these?

Darragh   I can do that.

Carol   No, you can't. You'll have a heart attack.

Claudia   What about my heart?

Carol   Your heart is fine.

Frank *stops playing, writes something down.*

Frank   I can help.

Carol (*handing her a banner that says '6 today!' or something*) Will you do this then, Mum? Frank, can you blow up the balloons?

Frank   Yes sir.

Darragh   And what will I do?

Carol   The candles are still out in the car, in the passenger door. Will you get those?

Darragh   I will.

Darragh *exits.*

Frank   I got those candles that don't go out when you blow them.

Claudia   Why would you do that?

Carol   To prolong the pain, mother. Will you get the cake?

Frank   I gave it to your mum.

Claudia   I have my own cake in the fridge.

Frank   She'll want the Iron Man one. No offence.

Carol *removes a load of tinsel stuff and throws it around the place.*

Carol   Mum threw that one out.

Claudia   What are you doing?

Frank   Did / you?

Carol   I'm decorating.

Frank *goes out to where* **Claudia** *threw out the cake.*

Claudia   You're making a mess.

Carol   It's meant to be thrown around.

Darragh *re-enters.*

Darragh   The keys of your car, Carol?

Claudia   Not all over the floor, it's meant / to be

Carol   Frank has them, Dad.

Frank *re-enters.*

Frank   There was still half of that Iron Man / cake left.

Claudia   Stop doing that.

Darragh   The keys, Frank?

Frank   What?

Darragh   Of the car.

Frank   I don't remember / having . . .

Claudia   Maybe as a centrepiece decoration . . .

Frank   Carol has / them

Claudia   . . . but not just thrown all about the place willy-nilly / like that

Carol   Has what?

Frank   The keys to the car, I gave them / to you

Carol   You didn't. I took Sarah out of the / back seat

Claudia   Carol?

Darragh   Would they be in the hall?

Frank   I did. I remember / handing them to you

Claudia   Carol, stop throwing that stuff / on the floor. It's desperate!

Carol   Mum, leave me –

Darragh   Would they be hung up in the hall?

Frank   No, I gave them to Carol.

Darragh (*going into the hall*)   I'll / have a look.

Carol   You didn't! You took the keys from me remember? They were in my mouth –

Frank   Did I?

Claudia   Will you just give that to me?

Darragh *comes back from the hall.*

Darragh   No.

Claudia   Carol, you're making such a / mess.

Carol   JESUS CHRIST MUM WILL YOU FUCKING STOP!

Silence, the rain picks up. It's ferocious for a while.

Darragh (*about the keys*)   Oh look, there they are. On the kitchen counter the whole time.

Frank   I'll run out with you.

Darragh *and* **Frank** *leave.*

Carol   Sorry. I'm sorry.

Claudia   –

Carol *is upset.*

What is it love?

Carol   Em. Just . . . What am I doing?

Claudia   You're decorating.

Carol   No. I mean . . . (*upset*)

Claudia   What is it?

Carol *tries to gather herself.* **Claudia** *picks up some of the tinsel from the floor.*

Carol   Last night, Frank –

Claudia   Yes?

Carol   He said that he could hear guilt in my voice.

Claudia   Guilt?

Carol   Yes.

Claudia   What do you have to feel guilty about?

Carol   I think he's talking about the surgery. The implant.

Claudia   I don't understand.

Carol   I think he feels like I've pushed for getting an implant because . . .

Carol *is upset again.*

Claudia   Oh, what love?

Carol   Because I can't connect with her.

Claudia   Oh that's not true love.

Carol   That's what he means, I think. About guilt.

Claudia   Of course you connect with her.

Carol   She's so desperate to get away from me all the time.

Claudia   It's a phase, children / can be

Carol   I see her with Frank. And with Marion.

Claudia   With Marion?

Carol   Yeah, they have this . . . easiness . . . and I – (*She's too upset.*)

Claudia   Oh love.

Carol   What if it is the wrong thing to do? The implant.

Claudia   Carol. You're her mother, you know what is best for her.

Carol   And now . . . on top of everything – Louise.

Claudia   What?

Carol   Louise is dead, Mum.

Claudia   Who told you that?

Marion *enters in a towel.*

Marion   Sorry, my clothes are in there.

Carol   Oh.

Marion (*to* **Carol**)   Are you alright?

Carol   I'm fine, yeah.

Marion   You're crying. What happened?

Carol   Nothing. Your phone buzzed when you were in the shower.

Marion   Oh.

Marion *goes to read the message on her phone.*

Carol   Frank told me. About Louise.

Claudia   Who told him?

Carol   Marion.

Claudia   Oh. Does your father know?

Carol   I don't think so, no.

Marion *comes back in, holding her phone.*

Marion   My friend in Sligo texted me back.

Carol   And can you go there?

Marion   She said no.

Scene Two

Later. Everyone is gathered around the birthday cake. The room is in darkness, lit only by the light of the candles. Perhaps there are party hats. **Marion** *signs the song, while the rest of the family sing.* **Frank** *accompanies on the piano . . .*

All
Happy Birthday to you!
Happy Birthday to you!
Happy Birthday dear Sarah!
Happy Birthday to you!

Carol   Blow out the candles.

Claudia   Come on, make a wish.

Carol   Okay. One. Two. Three. Blow!

Sarah *blows, the candles quench.*

All   Yay! Good girl. Etc.

The candles re-light, it's charming.

Claudia   Oh! Go again love!

Sarah *blows again, the candles quench, then re-light.*

Darragh   Why won't they go out?

Claudia   Frank got jokey ones that / re-light.

Carol   You have to put them in water to stop them.

Frank   Blow again!

Sarah *blows again, they quench then re-light.*

Darragh   Are you trying to torture the / child Frank?

Carol   This is insufferable, here –

Carol *removes the candles from the cake and puts them in a glass of water. Darkness.*

Frank   Sorry, I thought they would be a bit of / fun.

Darragh   Is someone turning on the lights?

Carol *turns the lights on.* **Sarah** *has left the room in the darkness.*

Frank   Oh, she's gone.

Claudia   Ah.

Beat.

Who is having cake then?

Carol   Sorry, Mum.

Frank   I'll take a slice.

Carol   Me too, looks yum.

Darragh (*holding up the gift*)   I wanted to give her my present.

Frank   From you?

Claudia   Yes from Darragh, but not from me. He's been very clear about that.

Carol   What is it?

Darragh   It's *Great Expectations*.

Marion (*signs*)   What?

Frank (*signs*)   Great (*spoken*) expectations?

Marion (*signs*)   Expectations.

Frank (*signs*)   *Great Expectations.*

Marion (*signs to* **Ciara**)   Book called / *Great Expectations.*

Darragh   By Charles Dickens. It's mine, published in the sixties.

Marion (*signs to* **Ciara**)   Go on.

Ciara *exits.*

Darragh   It's an abridged edition for children. It's old now, obviously.

Claudia   What made you think of that?

Carol   She's six, you know that right, Dad?

Darragh   There are pictures in it, Car, I'm not an idiot.

Frank   The sixties – can I see?

Darragh   My father used to read it to me when I was a boy. At bedtime.

Claudia   Oh, isn't that lovely, Car?

Darragh   I got a fright, as a child. And . . . couldn't sleep. Nightmares and that. The sound of my father's voice reading it – yeah, helped.

Carol   Ah, Dad.

Darragh   I'd like to read it to Sarah. Soon. When she can hear me.

Claudia *gives* **Darragh** *a kiss.*

Claudia   You're a big softie really.

Marion   What's the book about?

Darragh   You've never heard of *Great Expectations*?

Marion   I've heard of it, I just don't know the story.

Darragh   Well, it's very complicated.

Marion   That's okay. Try me.

Frank   It's about an orphan, right?

Darragh   Yes, called Pip. He wants to be . . . what would you call it . . . worthy of Estella, who is the adopted daughter of the eccentric spinster, Miss Havisham. They are well off. He's not.

Frank   If only he could be good enough for the rich girl. Am I right?

Carol   Zing.

Marion (*signed*)   What does that mean, spinster?

Frank (*signed*)   Like, woman on her own.

Claudia*'s phone rings.*

Claudia   Oh, that's Rita now. (*Answering.*) Hi Rita. Good, good / yeah. We're in the middle of the party now.

Marion   Is it like *Aladdin*?

Darragh   *Aladdin*?

Marion   Is Estella a princess?

Claudia (*on the phone*)   Fine, Yeah. We started late, it's been a / busy day, Rita.

Darragh   No, she's just . . . a rich person.

Marion   Ciara loves *Aladdin*.

Frank   It is *kind of* like *Aladdin*, in / a way.

Claudia (*on the phone*)   Oh, you saw her last night? Yes, she's a friend of Car and / Frank. I'll tell you about it again –

Carol   If you swap out London for Agrabah.

Frank   Agrabah!

Claudia (*on the phone*)   I did. Frank said he'd be delighted to.

Marion (*signs*)   What?

Frank (*signing*)   Nothing, just talking about *Aladdin*.

Claudia (*on the phone*)   Yeah, he said he'd talk to / you about that himself.

Darragh (*to* **Marion**)   Anyway, will I tell you how it ends?

Marion   Yes!

Carol   Spoiler alert.

Darragh   In the end Pip comes into money and finally pairs off with Estella.

Marion   He gets the girl?

Frank   I thought they parted ways in the end?

Darragh   That's one of the endings, yes. There are two.

Marion (*signs*)   I don't / understand?

Darragh   People fight over which ending is the definitive one. But, in my / version he meets Estella again and they are reconciled.

Frank (*signs*)   There are two different endings / to the book.

Claudia (*on the phone*)   I'm sure he can.

Marion (*signs*)   To this book?

Frank (*signs*)   Yeah. The one I read is where Pip doesn't end up with Estella, but in this one he does.

Marion (*signs*)   That's weird that there are two endings.

Carol   Stop doing that.

Frank   What?

Carol   Signing like that, it's rude.

Frank   I'm just explaining what we were talking about.

Claudia (*to* **Frank**)   Will you go over to Rita this evening?

Darragh   Explaining what?

Frank   That there are two different endings.

Claudia   Frank?

Frank (*to* **Claudia**)   Not this evening. Maybe / during the week –

Darragh   Is there something wrong with the ending?

Frank   No.

Carol   It's a lovely gift. Really. Thanks, Dad.

Claudia (*on the phone*)   He said / during the week.

Marion'*s phone dings. She has gotten a message.*

Claudia   She wanted to know if you would start this Wednesday? She has a / hair appointment –

Frank   Sarah's surgery is tomorrow so Wednesday / won't work.

Claudia (*on the phone*)   Oh, Rita! I'm not thinking, Sarah has her surgery tomorrow. I know. So / he'll be . . . yeah, I know, I know.

Marion   What about Miss Havisham?

Claudia   When will I say / Frank?

Darragh   Oh, she has a tragic end. No matter which version you read.

Frank   Sorry?

Marion   What happens?

Claudia   That you'll go over?

Frank   Next weekend, maybe.

Frank *cuts some cake for the children.*

Darragh   Her dress catches fire.

Claudia (*on the phone*)   Next weekend he said, Rita.

Marion   Fire?

Claudia (*on the phone*)   Alright, I'll tell him. Bye Rita. (*Hangs up.*)

Darragh   Yes. And she dies.

Claudia   Who dies?

Darragh   Miss Havisham.

Claudia   Oh.

Darragh   In the book. I was saying I'm going to read it to Sarah.

Claudia   I heard that part, yes.

Frank   Are you having cake Claudia?

Claudia   I'll do that.

Frank   Some for the girls here.

Marion (*taking the cake for the girls*)   I'll go.

Marion *exits.*

Frank   There's an inscription.

Claudia   What does it say?

Frank   Here, do you want to read it?

Darragh   'Sweet Darragh, all our love. Mummy and Daddy.' And then the date – August 8th, '65.

Darragh *is emotional.*

Claudia   Oh love.

Darragh   That's my father's handwriting, there.

Carol (*hugging him*)   Oh c'mere Dad, you big eejit.

Marion *enters. Her phone dings in her pocket and draws their attention.*

Marion   Sarah is quiet.

Carol   She's probably tired.

Marion   Do you think she's nervous?

Frank   About tomorrow?

Carol   She doesn't really know what is happening.

Frank   We've explained it to her, but . . .

Carol   She's only six.

Marion   What about you?

Carol   Us?

Marion   Are you nervous?

Frank   Yes.

Darragh   Why don't you have an implant for Ciara?

Marion   I decided not to.

Darragh   Are you against it?

Marion   No.

Darragh   Why not then?

Marion   Because I'm Deaf. She's Deaf. We're happy. I've got no reason to change anything.

Darragh   Would she not be better off?

Carol   Let's change the subject, please.

Claudia   Of course she would.

Marion   If Ciara wants one when she's older, she can get it.

Claudia   But, the thing is, her brain, it's better to get it when they're young. Isn't that it Carol?

Marion   Some of the older Deaf people are against it.

Darragh   Are they?

Marion   Yes.

Carol   Marion?

Marion (*signs*)   She told me to tell you positive things about the surgery.

Frank   Did you?

Carol   What?

Frank   Tell Marion to say positive things about the implant?

Carol (*to* **Marion**)   What are you doing?

Darragh   So, you're telling me that if this implant was available to the Deaf community fifty, sixty years ago that they wouldn't have gone for it?

Carol   Let's stop now. Change the subject.

Darragh   It would have made their lives a lot easier. And their families' lives. That's a fact.

Marion's *phone dings. Another message.* **Marion** *checks her phone.*

Frank   Did you, Car?

Claudia   I asked her Frank, just to reassure you. That's all.

Marion   Shit.

Marion *stands and walks to the study, texting. A silence.*

Darragh   I'm tired all of a sudden.

Claudia   Why don't you lie down for a bit.

Darragh   If I lie down, I won't sleep tonight.

Claudia   You don't sleep anyway.

Carol   Lie down if you're tired, Dad.

Darragh   Maybe I'll go for a walk.

Claudia   In that rain?

Darragh *goes to the cupboard, takes out the whiskey.*

Darragh   No. I just – need to get the blood moving.

Frank   Oh. Sorry about that, Darragh. We'll replace it.

Darragh (*pouring himself a glass*)   So, how *was* last night then Frank? What did you make of the surgeon?

Carol   Frank doesn't like him. They didn't hit it off.

Darragh   Doesn't matter if you like him. Can the man do his job properly? That's what matters.

Claudia   Exactly. People don't have to like you, Frank, do they? They just have to like your music – isn't that right?

Frank   I'm not boring holes into children's skulls with my music.

Darragh   That's debatable.

Claudia, Carol *and* **Darragh** *laugh.*

Darragh   Don't let your opinion of the man influence whether he can do his job Frank.

Frank   What is his job, then?

Darragh   To perform a surgery.

Frank   To what end?

Darragh   To cure her of her Deafness.

Frank   Don't say cure. I don't like that.

Claudia   What don't you like?

Frank   The word 'cure'. It's offensive.

Darragh   What should I say?

Frank   Do you think she needs to be cured?

Carol   He didn't mean it like that.

Frank   Okay. Then don't say 'cure'.

Marion's *phone dings.*

Darragh   A gift then. The surgeon will give her the gift of hearing. Is that better?

Claudia   A gift for her birthday. I like that.

Frank   Mm.

Claudia   She'll hear your voice. She'll be able to hear what we're saying.

Frank   Yeah.

Claudia   Hear her grandad reading to her.

Frank   Yeah.

Claudia   You need to think about what is best for Sarah.

Frank   Is it what's best though? I dunno.

Darragh   What's the alternative?

Frank   Sorry?

Darragh   Leave her the way she is?

Frank   Is there something wrong with the way she is?

Carol   Frank –

Frank   It's a very risky operation, Darragh.

Darragh   That's the price you have to pay so that she can be like the rest of us.

Frank   Graham described the process of inserting the steel into her cochlea. He said that it's like driving a JCB through a daisy field.

Carol   Ok –

Frank   That's how violent it is.

Claudia   You just don't like him that's all.

Frank   No, I don't.

Claudia   Are you being a bit sensitive, maybe?

Frank   Don't patronise me.

Darragh   Don't you –

Frank   He's talking about my daughter / Claudia . . .

Carol   Frank!

Frank   JCB in a daisy field . . . that's my little girl's brain he's talking about. The fucking cunt.

Darragh   Don't curse / like that.

Carol   Frank!

Frank   Talking about her brain like there's something / wrong with –

Darragh   This is my house. How dare you / curse like that –

Frank   And words like 'cure', anything that pushes you out of / your –

Carol   Stop! Both of you stop!

There is a silence. The rain pours outside. **Marion**'s *phone dings.*

Claudia   I'm going to have a glass of wine.

Claudia *stands.*

Does anyone want one?

Frank   Sorry. I'm sorry, Claudia, for raising my voice. Sorry, Darragh.

Darragh   That's / okay.

Frank   I'm sorry.

Claudia   Doesn't matter.

Marion's *phone dings again. She is reading the messages, visibly distressed. She re-enters.*

Marion   Em. I'm not sure what to do.

They look at her.

My boyfriend knows I'm here.

Carol   How?

Marion   I told him.

Claudia   What did he say?

Marion   He's pissed off. Said I made a fool of him earlier.

Carol   How?

Marion   At the pool, with you both. Everyone saw us.

Carol   Why would that make a fool of him?

Marion   He's coming here to get me.

Claudia   Here?

Marion (*signs*)   I have to go.

Darragh   What's happening?

Marion   Oh, em.

Silence.

I found out about your sister. Louise is dead. I'm sorry.

Silence.

Darragh   When?

Marion   A couple of years ago.

Silence.

Darragh   How?

Marion   Lung cancer.

Darragh   Okay.

Marion   She was a smoker. (*Beat.*) Sorry.

Marion's *phone dings, she looks at it.*

Darragh   Anything else?

Marion   She had a happy life, they said.

Darragh   Who did?

Marion   Her friends. There were a lot of people who loved her.

Darragh   Why didn't they tell me?

Marion   Deaf people here don't like this family.

Carol   Why?

The phone dings again. **Marion** *looks.*

Marion   I need to get Ciara.

Marion *goes out to get* **Ciara**. *Silence for a while.*

Darragh   I want to go to bed.

Carol   Mum?

Claudia   Then let's get you to bed.

Darragh   Why didn't anyone –

Claudia   It's okay, come on.

Claudia *takes* **Darragh** *to bed.* **Marion** *re-enters with* **Ciara**.

Carol   Did you know Louise?

Marion   No. My boyfriend's mum knew her. They played cards together.

Darragh (*shouts, off*)   I told you. You said she was going to – (*Beat.*) You didn't do it. And now look – now I –

Frank *and* **Carol** *look out to the hallway.*

Carol   Can you tell me about my aunt?

Marion   I need to go.

Carol   Please? I don't know anything about her.

Marion   Will you talk for me?

Frank *speaks this as* **Marion** *signs it to him.*

Marion (*signs*)   This is just what I was told. When Louise was . . . four years old her parents sent her to the Deaf school in Cabra. She was a boarder even though they lived here. There was a lot of abuse, rotten.

Marion's *phone dings.*

(*Signs*.) Louise ran away from school a few of times, here, but her mother and father sent her back. She wrote letters to Darragh about what was happening but she heard nothing. Then, when she was about 10, I think, something really bad happened to her. My boyfriend's mum told me this. She said Louise had been badly beaten or something more – I don't know. She wouldn't say exactly, but that's what I felt she meant.

Carol   Jesus.

Marion (*signs*)   She ran home and when she arrived at the door, here, your grandfather wouldn't let her in. He phoned the police. And the police took her back to the school. After that . . . she never saw any of them again. Finished. She wrote letters to Darragh after she left the school to explain what happened – but she heard nothing. All the Deaf people know the story.

Marion's *phone dings, she looks at it*.

Marion   Shit. I really have to go.

Frank   Where will you go?

Marion (*signs to* **Sarah**)   Say bye-bye to me. I love you. (*Spoken*.) Oh, here's your charger.

Frank   Can I bring you somewhere?

Marion   No. Thanks.

Carol *takes the charger from* **Marion**. **Marion**, **Ciara**, **Frank** *exit. We hear the front door close*. **Carol** *is alone for a while*.

The rain.

Claudia *enters. She fills her wine glass*.

Carol   Is Dad alright?

Claudia   No.

Carol   Will I go up to him?

Claudia   Just leave him alone now.

Carol   Is he in bed?

Claudia   No. He's staring out the window. At her.

Carol   Marion?

Claudia   I wish she wouldn't stand out in the square like that.

Carol   Where is she supposed to stand?

Claudia   Anywhere else but right there in front of us.

Beat.

Carol   Marion told us about Louise.

Claudia   Did she?

Carol   What Granny and Grandad did to her.

Claudia   What did they do?

Carol   They told the guards to take her away. When she ran home from school. Did you know all of this?

Claudia   Your father told me a little.

Carol   Marion said she was badly beaten, and that they phoned the guards on her.

Claudia   Is that what she said?

Carol   She was ten years old. Is that true, Mum?

Claudia *pulls a chair from the table over to a high cupboard and takes down a tin box.*

What are you doing?

Claudia   Your father was digging in the garden for it earlier.

Carol   For what?

Claudia   This. The letters. I found them years ago.

Carol   Why didn't you give them to him?

Claudia   They are very upsetting.

Carol   What do they say?

Claudia   Terrible things.

Silence.

Carol, your grandparents weren't bad people, you know that. It was a different time. They did what they thought was best. To protect your father.

Carol   From what?

Claudia   And it's my duty to protect you. All of you.

Carol   Mum?

Claudia   You understand that. I know you do.

Claudia *takes the box out of the house to dump them.* **Carol** *is alone. After a few moments,* **Claudia** *re-enters.*

Claudia   She's gone.

Carol   Marion?

Claudia   Yes.

Carol   Did her boyfriend get her?

Claudia   I have no idea.

Claudia *finishes her glass of wine, then puts it in the sink.*

Anyway. Doesn't matter.

Claudia *exits.*

Act Three

Frank *is playing music at the piano. The laptop is open beside him playing the footage from* **Sarah**'*s birthday at the pool silently on the screen.* **Carol** *enters.*

Carol   I'm going to bed.

He keeps playing.

Frank, I'm talking to you.

Frank *stops playing. There is just the sound of the rain.*

Frank   The morning of Sarah's first consultation the doctor was surprised at / how old

Carol   Graham, is that who you're talking about?

Frank   Yes. He said that he was surprised that Sarah was so old.

Carol   The aim is to intervene at infancy / now

Frank   He was saying that it would be very unusual for him or Dr Walsh / to

Carol   Laura.

Frank   Jesus, Carol, I get it. You know all of their first names. They're called Dr this and Dr that to me, okay?

Carol   Okay.

Frank   He said it was unusual to go ahead with an implant at Sarah's age. That she may not benefit. And I felt relieved.

He looks at **Carol**. *Nothing.*

When I was telling Sarah, trying to let her know that it might not go ahead, she . . . made this heart-breaking little frown. All these heavy thoughts . . . like she had failed. And em, I never want her to think she's not good enough.

Carol   Frank.

Frank   So when they said they would 'give her a chance'.

Carol   That's a good / thing.

Frank   I didn't realise she needed / one

Carol   This is the right / decision.

Frank   Shut up for a second, Carol.

Silence.

It's disgusting. What happened to your aunt. What they did. You –

Carol   Don't talk to me like that.

Frank   It makes me –

Carol   Don't tell me to shut up.

Beat.

Frank   Sorry.

Silence.

Marion asked me something the other day, caught me off guard. She asked if Sarah would leave the Deaf school, go somewhere else. A mainstream school.

Carol   Oh.

Frank   I didn't realise what she was asking at the time.

Carol   I suppose she's thinking about Ciara, and the friendship there.

Frank   Yeah.

Beat.

Frank   And will she? Go to another school?

Carol   I don't know.

Frank   That's what I said.

Carol   She probably won't . . . I don't know.

Frank   I got the impression Marion thinks she will leave.

Carol   Oh.

Frank   Sarah and Ciara get on, they're friends.

Carol   I know.

Frank   So.

Carol   I'd prefer if we, em . . . didn't . . . if that's okay?

Frank   Didn't what?

Carol   If we do, I mean . . . Nothing to do with . . . it's just . . . what is best.

Frank   Oh, so you do want her to leave the school then?

Carol   She'll have to focus on listening and speech so . . .

Frank   So?

Carol   So, it's not useful for her to use sign. While her brain . . . you know, adjusts and –

Frank   She'll sign with her friends if she's at the school.

Carol   Which isn't helpful, so . . . em. Yes, then. I'd be of the opinion that leaving the school is what's best.

Frank   I'd like if she stayed connected with the Deaf kids and that . . . community.

Carol   I think you're putting too much importance on this idea of her as a Deaf girl. I don't think that it's useful. We're making her life better.

Frank   Are we though?

Carol   Of course we are! Being able to hear is better than being deaf, Frank.

Frank She's happy.

Carol We have to help her succeed, be the best.

Frank Is that what it's about?

Carol Opportunity. Her potential to thrive. Yes.

Frank No, you said to be the best.

Carol I meant in the way / that . . .

Frank Like becoming a doctor?

Carol What's best for *her*, is what I mean.

Frank Not what's best for you?

Carol –

Silence.

Frank Were you not happy when we were in town?

Carol I was happy.

Frank Were we not succeeding?

Carol Can we stop – I'm exhausted.

Frank Was there something wrong with our life before?

Carol Frank, come on, this feels like a trap.

Frank Answer

Carol It just wasn't . . .

Frank Yes?

Carol . . . good enough. Was it?

Frank When she was born, we both said 'she's perfect'.

Carol Aha, the trap.

Frank Was she perfect?

Carol That's not fair.

Frank   Answer me. Was she perfect?

Carol   This is cruel. What you're doing.

Frank   What am I doing?

Carol   Making me feel so fucking . . . (*screams*) guilty.

Frank   –

Carol   I have nothing to feel guilty about!

Sarah *enters and stands in the doorway. She is holding a plastic cup.*

She is my daughter. Mine. Do you understand that?

Silence.

I am her mother.

Frank   Sarah!

Carol   Oh sweetheart, what / are you doing up so late?

Frank   Do you want a drink of water?

Sarah *nods.*

Come on, love.

Frank *takes the cup, fills it with water.*

Carol   I'll bring you sweetheart, Daddy is busy here.

Frank   It's okay, I'll go.

Frank *and* **Sarah** *exit.* **Carol** *presses the space bar on the laptop.*

Frank
I am watching you
love!
I am watching,
I'm here.

Carol *presses the space bar again.* **Frank** *enters.*

Carol   Sorry. I'm sorry.

Frank   Me too.

Carol   For getting so angry. I'm just . . .

Frank   Yeah, I know.

Carol *looks at the video on the screen.*

Carol   That's the footage from the pool earlier?

Frank   Yeah. Your mum said something about it being like a silent film, when we turned off the volume. About all Sarah's memories being silent.

Carol   Oh.

Frank   Her memories so far . . . so –

Carol   You're going to . . . what? Add music to them?

Frank   Maybe. Yeah, I dunno. It's an idea. I'll film some more over the next while.

Carol (*about the sheet music*)   I see my name here.

Frank   Well, you're in the footage so.

Carol   Oh? So now I'm a character in your opera?

Frank   You, Sarah and me – so far. I'm, just trying something.

Carol   A family drama.

Beat. **Frank** *plays a chord on the piano, the beginning of the opera.*

Carol   What were you trying to say, earlier?

Frank   I'm not sure.

Carol   Do you not want to go ahead with the operation?

Frank   No, it's not –

Carol   Because if you don't want to, if you really / feel –

Frank   I do want to, I just – I'm afraid, I think.

Carol   Yeah, me too.

Frank   Of doing the wrong thing, hurting her.

Carol   Frank.

Frank   I'm afraid of what she'll hear.

Beat.

Carol   Sometimes, Frank. You can be a little dramatic, the way you speak.

Frank   What?

Carol   I'm afraid of what she'll hear. That's a little dramatic.

Frank   I'm afraid she'll hear how we speak to each other. That we don't . . .

Carol   . . . love each other. Is that what you were going to say?

Frank   No. I was going to say we don't know what we're doing.

Carol   Oh.

Frank   I do love you, Carol.

Carol   –

Frank   Why did you say that? I do –

Carol   I know. It's okay.

A silence. Then **Frank** *plays again.*

It's good. Your idea for the opera.

Frank   Thanks.

Carol   Very heroic.

Beat.

I'm glad you've settled on something.

Frank   Yeah.

Carol   Are you going to work some more?

Frank   Just a little, then I'll come up.

Carol   Okay.

Carol *gives* **Frank** *a kiss on the forehead.*

Night.

Carol *exits.* **Frank** *plays the piano. The house is torn open, and the opera is inserted into it.*

Opera

1

Sarah's birthday at the swimming pool. There are other Deaf children at the pool. Sarah is looking around trying to see where Frank and Carol are.

Carol
Sarah?

Frank
Sarah?

Carol & Frank
We're here!

Frank
Sarah! We're here! Look!

Carol
Look love! We're right here!

Sarah sees her parents, she's reassured.

Frank
So. Don't look now. That's Marion's boyfriend.
Standing there.

Carol
The lifeguard?

Frank
Yes. Him there.

Carol
He's looking at us.

Frank
That's why I said don't look. Jesus. It's awkward now.

Carol
He seems really . . . / weird

Frank
Angry

Carol
. . . with us.

Lifeguard
Hey! Come on everyone. Look at me.
Come here! Look at me.

Carol
Oh. He's doing the cake.

Frank
Maybe he's pissed off because we asked him to do a cake?

Carol
No

Frank
It might be against the rules.

The children start to gather.

Take a photo Frank.

Frank
I'm filming it.

Carol
Right now?

Frank
Since a few minutes ago, yeah.

Carol
That'll be a long video.

Frank
Your mum might want to see it.

Carol
A feature film of children in a pool. Yeah,
I'm sure Mum will be delighted.

Frank
Sarah? Sarah? Sarah?

Frank & Carol
Sarah? Sarah? Look!

Lifeguard
Please be careful. Please stand back from the edge.
Be careful. Safety first. Remember the sign.

The **Lifeguard** *points at the sign.*

Please watch me carefully. Hey you, not you, the girl beside
you. Yes you. Watch me carefully. Come here, come over
here. Watch me. I said stand still. There. Okay? Ready.

The **Lifeguard** *starts the song in Sign Language. The Deaf
girls and boys join. A* **Second Lifeguard** *hands a cake to the*
Lifeguard.

All
Happy Birthday to you.
Happy Birthday to you.
Happy Birthday dear Sarah.
Happy Birthday to you.

Lifeguard
Come on Sarah, blow out the candles.

Sarah *looks at* **Frank** *and* **Carol.**

Frank & Carol
Blow! Big deep breath! Blow!

Sarah *blows the candles out! All the children and the*
Lifeguard *Deaf clap.*

Lifeguard
Happy?

Carol
What did he say?

Frank

He asked if we are happy. Yes.

Both

Yes. Yes!

*The **Lifeguard** looks to **Frank**. Putting on a show of niceness.*

Lifeguard

Are you finished?

Frank

We're good.

Carol

We have everything we want.

Lifeguard

Okay then. Everyone! Let's get in to the water! Please be careful! Watch the edges. Slowly. Slowly! Don't get hurt!

*The **Lifeguard** throws multi-coloured little paddle boards into the pool, one for each child. It's playful. The children grab the paddle boards, and then splash their way around the pool.*

Lifeguard

Hold on tight. Kick your legs. Head down in the water. Remember to breathe all the time. Use your legs and kick! Kick! Kick!

*The water from the children kicking is like mini explosives everywhere. **Sarah** hesitates at the pool side. She looks at **Frank**.*

Frank

It's okay. Go ahead now. It's fine. I am watching you love! I am watching, I'm here.

*We hear **Frank** laughing. **Carol**'s phone rings.*

Carol

Shit, that's my phone – sorry. That's Mum (*answering the phone*). Hi Mum, we're at the pool, it's really noisy here. What? – Because you were asleep . . . They've just done a

cake. Yeah, we brought a cake for her. To have with her
friends . . . The kids . . . here. She just blew out
the candles. It was really nice.

Frank
Tell her I'll bring the cake home.

Carol
It's an Iron Man cake. Yes.

Sarah *waves at* **Frank.**

Frank
Yes! I can see you love. Jump again / I am watching you

Carol
Frank is filming her.

Frank
Look at her Car!

Carol
No, it's not weird. I know it's a public / pool Mum

Frank
It's fine. / I'm filming my daughter's birthday. Tell her –

Carol
I have to go Mum.

Sarah *looks at* **Frank** *and* **Carol.**

Sarah (*not sung, just signed*)
Did you see me?

Frank & Carol
Yes, we saw you.

Frank
I thought you were brilliant!

Carol's *phone rings again, we see her pull it out of her bag
and look at the screen.*

Carol

Oh shit Frank, I've to take this, it's the hospital.
I'll be two seconds.

Carol *walks away from* **Frank. Sarah** *watches her go.* **Sarah** *is looking at* **Frank.**

Frank

It's okay love. Go and join your friends. I'm here,
I'm watching you! Go on. Ready. Steady.

2

Sarah *in a hospital bed, pre-operation, watching an iPad.*
Carol *is sitting on the bed with her,* **Frank** *is standing next to it.* **Graham** *is about to leave the room.*

Frank

Wait. I've got a question. Please wait.

Graham

Are you filming me?

Carol

It's for his opera. The commission, remember?
You don't mind, do you?

Graham

I thought the opera was about war?

Frank

It's evolving.

Graham

Okay. What's the question?

Frank

Can I ask you about music? About
when she can listen to music?

Graham

She can listen to music whenever she wants to –
After we have switched her on, of course. However,

I will say manage your expectations. The sensations,
the complexity, the range of sounds in music – well,
the implant can struggle with all of that.

Frank
What do you mean?

Graham
Music can sound tinny, robotic, unpleasant, sometimes,
through the implant. No nuance. She won't hear music
like you do, you know. But, I mean, what is music really?
It's all subjective, isn't it? Look, the implant functions
best within the parameters of speech. Speaking voices.
Like us right now / talking

Carol
Talking, yes. She'll hear our voices.

Graham
Exactly. That's what we're aiming for. Voices.
Words. Sentences. Music is tricky. Like I said, sometimes
tinny, robotic. It lives in the grey area. Honestly, we
don't know, really, what she'll hear. Remember she's
never heard anything, at all before this. So, it's all to
play for, you know. She's still young.

Carol
Thanks Graham. He's just a bit worried.

Frank
Are you not a bit worried?

Graham
Let's try and be optimistic, mum and dad, shall we?

Carol
Thanks so much for everything.

Frank
And – if it doesn't work. The implant – when do we know?

Graham
Let's cross that bridge. If we come to it.

Frank

Answer the question. Please.

Carol

Frank, just say thank you and let the man get / ready

Graham

We won't know if the surgery has been a success until after
her 'switch on'. Three weeks from now. If the implant can
bring sound to the Deaf child's brain then, we're gravy.

Frank

And what about injury during surgery?
Tissue damage, facial nerves?

Graham

She's in safe hands. I'm pretty good at my job, I promise.

Frank

She's my daughter.

Graham

You just have to trust me.

Carol

Let him go Frank.

Graham

Don't sweat it pal. Maybe go for a walk. Help you calm down.

Frank

Wait. Ah. I've got another question / about

Carol

Frank, stop. Let the man go. Sorry. Sorry.

3

Post-surgery. **Sarah** *is in the hospital bed, asleep or drowsy.*

Graham

All smiles mum and dad. Let the first thing she sees be
big, bright smiles. She'll be relying on you for that.

Frank

Oh.

Graham

She'll be very drowsy and weepy. That's normal.
Try not to be upset in front of her.

Sarah *moves a little.*

Frank

Hi love. It's all over. It's all over now.

Carol

Hi my little darling. You're such a brave girl.

Graham

She's not really very alert at the moment.
It's an intense surgery. Let her rest.

Frank

Everything was okay?

Graham

Perfect, just like I said. There was no need to worry.

Carol

Thank you.

Graham

What does she need?

Frank & Carol

Big smiles.

Carol

We're so grateful. Thank you so, so, so, so much.

Graham *leaves.*

It's all over now, love. She's okay. We can breathe.

4

A new swimming pool. **Sarah** *is at the edge of the water with her bandage in a waterproof covering.* **Carol** *is also in a swimsuit, sitting beside her.* **Sarah** *looks at her father.*

Sarah
Jump?

Frank
No. I told you. Just your feet. For now.
Paddle your feet. You cannot jump yet.

Carol
Incy Wincy Spider. Climbed up the water spout

Sarah
Why?

Frank
Soon. I promise. Soon.

Darragh *swims to* **Sarah***'s feet, stands in the water and joins in with* **Carol.**

Carol
Down came the rain

Carol & Darragh
And washed the spider out

Sarah
Where is Ciara?

Frank
Ciara is not here. She swims at a different pool now.

Carol & Darragh
Out came the sunshine. And dried up all the rain

Sarah
Why?

Carol & Darragh
And Incy Wincy Spider. Climbed up the spout again

Frank
Look. Mummy is singing a song to you.
About a spider. And Grandad too.

Sarah
Why?

5

The audiology room in the hospital. This is **Sarah**'s *'switch on'. The* **Audiologist** *wants to see the implant.*

Audiologist
Can I look? Good girl. It's ok.

Sarah *tries to push the* **Audiologist** *away.* **Frank** *and* **Carol** *try to support.*

Just give her some space mum and dad. She just needs some
space now. You can hold her hand, mum, if you need to.

The **Audiologist** *slides a piece of paper and a red marker in front of* **Sarah**.

Dad, can you sign this for her please?

Frank *comes into view.*

Audiologist
Sarah?

Frank
Sarah?

Audiologist
When you hear a sound, please put a dot on
the page with the marker. The red marker.

Frank
When you hear a sound, put a dot on the page.
With the marker. The red one.

Audiologist

Ok?

Frank

Yes , she understands.

Audiologist

Alright everyone. I'm going to switch her on.

The device is switched on, **Sarah** *shudders as she hears sound for the first time. A sonic change. From here onwards everything that is sung and spoken is heard as if through a cochlear implant.*

Audiologist

Ba Ba Ba Ba Ba Ba Ba Ba

Sarah *recognises the sound.*

She can hear that.

Ba Ba Ba Ba Ba Ba Ba Ba Ba Ba

Sarah *puts a dot on the page.*

Frank

Oh my god.

Carol

Oh sweetheart.

Audiologist

Ba Ba Ba Ba Ba Ba Ba Ba Ba Ba

Carol

Sarah? Sarah? Look at Mummy.

Sarah *puts another dot on the page.*

Mummy loves you. Oh, this is incredible.

Audiologist

Ba Ba Ba Ba Ba Ba Ba Ba Ba Ba

This is a great sign. The electrodes are working.
Let's test for pitch.

Ba Ba Ba Ba Ba Ba Ba Ba Ba Ba

Sarah *puts another dot on the page.*

Frank
Sarah? Sarah? Look at Daddy. Sarah,
I'm here. Sarah? Sarah?

Carol
Sarah? Sarah? Look at me Sarah?

Frank
Can you hear my voice? Sarah, it's Daddy.

Carol
Sarah?

Audiologist
Ba Ba Ba Ba Ba Ba Ba Ba Ba Ba

Carol
Mummy loves you!

Frank
Sarah? Sarah? Look at Daddy. Sarah, Sarah? I'm here.

Sarah *looks at her father. We can see that she's a little
uncomfortable.*

Frank
She's smiling. You're smiling darling. Sarah? Are you happy?

Audiologist
She looks happy.

Carol
She looks so happy.

Frank
She's smiling.

Audiologist
She's smiling for daddy.

It becomes a little bit too much.

Okay

She might need a break.

Carol
She's such a brave girl.

Frank
We're so proud of you love.

Audiologist
Good girl.

Frank
Sarah?

Carol
Are you alright love?

Audiologist
Let's just test one more thing.

Ba Ba Ba Ba Ba Ba Ba Ba Ba Ba Ba

Frank (*joins*)
Ba Ba Ba Ba Ba Ba Ba Ba Ba Ba Ba

Carol (*joins*)
Ba Ba Ba Ba Ba Ba Ba Ba Ba Ba Ba

All Voices
Ba Ba Ba Ba Ba Ba Ba Ba Ba Ba Ba

Scene Two

The evening of **Sarah**'s *'switch on'. Everything we hear in the following scene is still processed through the implant.* **Darragh**, **Claudia**, **Frank** *and* **Carol** *are watching* **Sarah**. **Sarah** *is irritated by her cochlear implant so she removes it.*

Silence.

Frank *goes to her and places the implant back on her head.*

Frank   Sarah. You need to leave it on, love.

Sarah *runs to* **Carol**. **Carol** *bends down to her, holds her. The dynamic is changed.*

Carol   She's not used to it, that's all.

Claudia   Is it a bit heavy for her, maybe?

Frank   Sarah love?

Carol   Don't show any panic, Frank, she'll react to that.

Darragh   Sarah?

Sarah *looks at* **Darragh**.

She heard me.

Claudia   She heard you, Dar.

Darragh   Can you hear me?

Claudia   Can you hear me, love?

Darragh   She can.

Claudia   Oh, isn't that just –

Frank   Sarah?

Carol   Okay, let's give it a rest. Let's not freak her out.

Claudia   Oh, Dar.

Frank   Sarah?

Darragh   Will you come with me? I'll bring her up to bed.

Darragh *picks up the copy of* Great Expectations, *takes* **Sarah***'s hand and leads her out of the room. The sound is no longer processed through the implant.*

Claudia   Everything worked out perfectly in the end. That's all that matters, isn't it?

Frank *and* **Claudia** *don't respond.* **Claudia** *exits.* **Carol** *takes out a glass and pours some wine.* **Frank** *takes out his phone to look at what he has recorded, and we hear:*

Audiologist
Can I look?
Good girl.
It's ok.

Just give her some space
mum and dad.
She just needs
some space now.

Frank *puts his earphones on, continues watching the footage.*
Silence.

End of play.

Acknowledgements

I am deeply grateful to everyone who supported and encouraged the development and production of this play.

Thank you to my family – Susan, Bernard and Aoife – for your boundless generosity, and for inspiring this work in the first place.

To my husband Paul – thank you for pushing me when I needed a push, holding me when I needed to be held, and knowing the difference between the two.